10 Minute Guide to Lotus® Notes 4.5

by Sue Plumley

A Division of Macmillan Computer Publishing
201 West 103rd St., Indianapolis, Indiana 46290 USA

I dedicate this book to Martha O'Sullivan and her family.

International Standard Book Number: 0-7897-0945-7
Library of Congress Catalog Card Number: 96-70615

98 97 8 7 6 5

Interpretation of the printing code: the rightmost double-digit number is the year of the book's first printing; the rightmost single-digit number is the number of the book's printing. For example, a printing code of 96-1 shows that this copy of the book was printed during the first printing of the book in 1996.

Printed in the United States of America

Publisher Roland Elgey
Vice President and Publisher Marie Butler-Knight
Publishing Director Lynn E. Zingraf
Marketing Director Lynn E. Zingraf
Editorial Services Director Elizabeth Keaffaber
Managing Editor Michael Cunningham
Acquisitions Editor Martha O'Sullivan
Product Development Specialist John Gosney
Production Editor Katie Purdum
Technical Editors Debbie Lynd, Jane Calabria
Technical Specialist Herb Feltner
Book Designer Barbara Kordesh
Cover Designer Dan Armstrong
Indexer CJ East
Production Team Lori Cliburn, Tricia Flodder, Diana Groth, Christopher Morris, Christy Wagner

Special thanks to Discovery Computing, Inc. for ensuring the technical accuracy of this book.

Contents

INTRODUCTION

Lotus Domino provides a powerful, yet easy-to-use electronic mail system, numerous features for sharing files and data with coworkers, methods for working remotely, and many other features that enable you to perform tasks over a network. Domino provides accessibility and flexibility and is suitable for large and small business systems.

Disclaimer:

Lotus, with the introduction of this product version, is now calling the former Notes Server software Domino. Additionally, Lotus has named the Notes product, in general, Domino. The Notes client, however, will still be called Notes. Because this book was written about the Notes client, I've used the term Notes throughout when referring to the product.

THE WHAT AND WHY OF LOTUS DOMINO AND NOTES

Whether you're a member of a small office or a large multi-building corporation, Domino can help you complete your work efficiently and quickly. For example, using the Notes client, you can do all of these things:

- Access document databases containing such company documents as forms, reports, lists, articles, and other information
- Create document databases to post to the network and share with coworkers
- Access databases your coworkers create and post to the network
- Send and receive e-mail within your company and between other computers attached to your company's network
- Attach files to e-mail, as well as import and export files to your e-mail messages to take full advantage of Notes' capabilities

Because the Lotus Notes client can accomplish so much, you might think it will be hard to use. Not so. Lotus Notes runs in Windows 95 (or OS/2, Windows NT or Windows 3.11, UNIX, or on the Macintosh) as a graphical user interface (GUI). A *GUI* (such as Windows) provides a graphical workspace that is easy to use and easy to understand. Lotus Notes takes advantage of that workspace. In addition, Notes is similar to other Lotus products in that it uses SmartIcons as tool buttons, InfoBoxes to represent related options, and other on-screen tools that you might already be familiar with.

Graphical User Interface A GUI (pronounced "gooey") makes interacting with your computer easy. You usually use a mouse to point at and select icons (small pictures that most often represent files or application programs), and you choose operations (commands from menus) to perform on those icons. A GUI is an alternative to a command-line interface, such as DOS, in which you enter text commands from the keyboard.

Why use Lotus Notes? Lotus Notes makes doing your everyday work faster and easier by enabling you to do the following things:

- Write and send messages to your coworkers without leaving your desk.
- Read, print, and answer messages from others in your organization.
- Attach files, import files, and export files to coworkers.
- Access databases of information and data supplied by your company and coworkers.
- Make your own documents available on the network for others to access.
- Join online discussion groups to get immediate feedback to your ideas.

Lotus Notes is fast, easy, and fun to learn, and all you have to invest is a little effort. You'll be pleased with the advantages and benefits you receive from the program.

Although this book concentrates on using Notes on a Windows 95 workstation, the procedures for most tasks are the same for OS/2, Windows NT, Macintosh, and so on.

WHY THE *10 MINUTE GUIDE TO LOTUS NOTES 4.5*?

The *10 Minute Guide to Lotus Notes 4.5* can save even more of your precious time. Each lesson is designed to be completed in 10 minutes or less, so you'll be up to snuff in basic Notes skills quickly.

Though you can jump around between lessons, starting at the beginning is a good plan. The bare-bones basics are covered first, and more advanced topics are covered later. The Appendix covers how to install the client software on either an OS/2 or Windows 95 workstation. And be sure to check out the inside front and back covers for a quick reference listing of all the Notes SmartIcons.

CONVENTIONS USED IN THIS BOOK

To help you move through the lessons easily, these conventions are used:

On-screen text	On-screen text appears in bold type.
What you type	Information you type appears in bold colored type.
Items you select	Commands, options, and icons you select or keys you press appear in colored type.

In telling you to choose menu commands, this book uses the format *menu title, menu command*. For example, the statement "choose File, Properties" means to "open the File menu and select the Properties command."

In addition to these conventions, the *10 Minute Guide to Lotus Notes 4.5* uses the following icons to identify helpful information:

Plain English New or unfamiliar terms are defined in (you got it) "plain English."

Timesaver Tips Look here for ideas that cut corners and confusion.

Panic Button This icon identifies areas where new users often run into trouble, and offers practical solutions to those problems.

This icon points out areas in Notes that will be different when the program is used on NT Workstation 4.

ACKNOWLEDGMENTS

A lot of hard work went into completing this project, and I'd like to thank all of those involved. First and foremost, my gratitude goes to my acquisitions editor, Martha O'Sullivan. Martha's efficiency, planning, and hard work make writing for her a pleasure. Thanks too to the product development specialist, John Gosney, whose suggestions and advice were, as always, invaluable. I'd also like to thank the production editor, Katie Purdum, for her guidance and attention to detail. Finally, thanks to Discovery Computing, Inc., for ensuring the technical consistency and accuracy of this book.

TRADEMARKS

LESSON 1

NAVIGATING NOTES

In this lesson, you learn to start and exit Notes, identify elements on the Notes workspace, and use the mouse and keyboard.

STARTING NOTES

You start Notes from the Windows 95 desktop. After starting Notes, you can leave it on-screen, or you can minimize the Notes window so it's easy to access anytime during your workday.

To start Lotus Notes, follow these steps:

1. From the Windows 95 desktop, select the Start button.
2. Choose Programs, Lotus Applications, Notes. (If Notes is not in the Lotus Applications folder, it will be in whichever folder you specified during installation.) The Choose Location dialog box appears unless your Notes program is automatically set up for network operation.

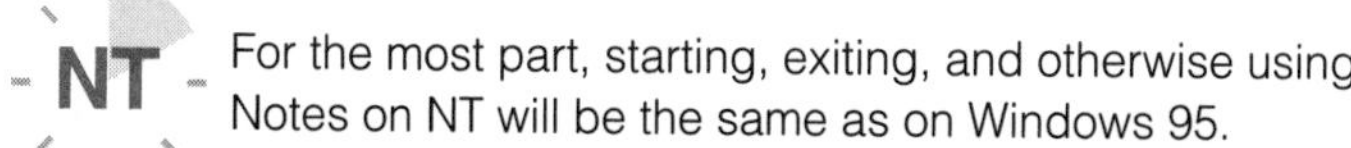

For the most part, starting, exiting, and otherwise using Notes on NT will be the same as on Windows 95.

3. Choose from the following options in the Current Location list:

   Home (Modem) Use this option when you're not connected by cable to the network and you plan to use a modem and telephone lines instead to connect to the network.

Island (Disconnected) Use this option when you plan to work in Notes but you don't plan to connect to the network during the session.

Office (Network) Use this option when you're connected to the network with cables.

Travel (Modem) Use this option when you're not connected by cable to the network and you plan to use a modem and phone line to connect instead. (The major difference between the Travel and Home locations is in how you set phone numbers and dialing options.)

This book assumes you're connecting using the Office (Network) option; however, most procedures and tasks are similar no matter which location option you choose. The Notes window appears (see Figure 1.1).

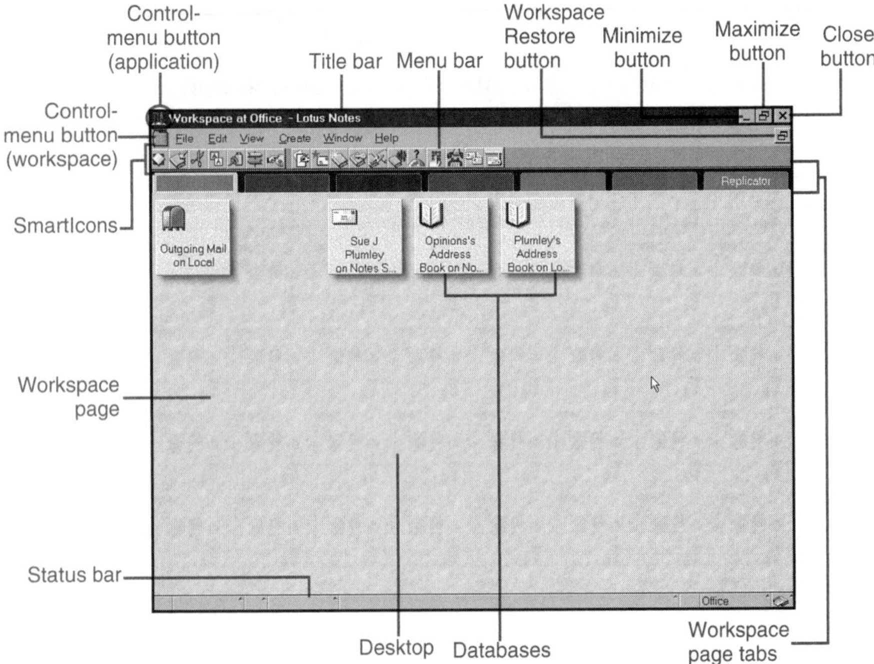

FIGURE 1.1 The Lotus Notes main window.

UNDERSTANDING THE NOTES WORKSPACE

Think of a workspace as a file cabinet drawer that holds all of the data you need to complete your work at the office. Other workspace "drawers" hold the data you need when traveling, when at home, or when disconnected from the network completely. The data within a workspace consists of information databases, mail, documents you create, and documents you copy from the network, as well as various other articles you may collect to complete your work.

Each item you see in the Notes workspace has a function that helps you navigate the Notes window and complete your work efficiently. Table 1.1 describes the elements of the Notes window.

TABLE 1.1 NOTES WINDOW ELEMENTS

ELEMENT	DESCRIPTION
Control-menu button (application)	Provides such commands as Move, Size, Minimize, and Close, with which you control the application window.
Control-menu button (workspace)	Provides such commands as Move, Size, Minimize, and Close, with which you control the workspace window.
Maximize button	Enlarges the Notes window to cover the Windows 95 desktop; when the window is maximized, the Maximize button changes to a Restore button that you can click to return the window to its previous size.

continues

TABLE 1.1 CONTINUED

ELEMENT	DESCRIPTION
Minimize button	Reduces the Notes window to a button on the taskbar; to restore the window to its original size, click the button on the taskbar.
Workspace Restore button	Returns the maximized workspace window to its previous size; when the workspace window is restored, you can display other workspace windows in the application window.
Close (X) button	Closes the Notes program.
Title bar	Contains the name of the current workspace and the program's name; also displays a description of selected menu commands.
Menu bar	Contains the menus you use to perform tasks in Notes.
SmartIcons	Enable you to perform tasks quickly by clicking the mouse on an icon in the SmartIcon bar.
Workspace page tabs	Enable you to change pages within the workspace; click a page tab to change to that page.
Workspace page	Holds databases and other information you want to store.
Databases	Contain collections of documents relating to the same topic; double-click a database to open it.

ELEMENT	DESCRIPTION
Mouse pointer	Enables you to access menus and perform tasks.
Status bar	Presents information about the selected item.

Workspace Pages Each workspace contains six pages you can use to organize databases. Databases contain documents and data that you create, import, copy, or otherwise access from the network.

USING THE MOUSE

You use the mouse to perform many actions in Lotus Notes. You can use the mouse to select items, open databases and other files, or move items, for example. After you select an item, you can perform another task on that item, such as copying, moving, or deleting it. Performing actions with a mouse is a matter of pointing, clicking, and double-clicking.

Selecting with the mouse involves two steps: pointing and clicking. To *point* to an object (an icon or a menu, for example), move the mouse across your desk or mouse pad until the on-screen mouse pointer touches the object. You can pick up the mouse and reposition it if you run out of room on your desk.

To *click*, position the mouse pointer on the object you want to select, and then press and release the left mouse button. Clicking an object selects it; the selected object becomes highlighted. A selected button (on the taskbar, for example) looks as if it's pressed in. When a button looks raised, it's deselected.

To *double-click* on an item, you point to the item and press and release the left mouse button twice quickly. Double-clicking is often a shortcut to performing a task. For example, you can open a database by double-clicking on its icon.

You can also use the mouse to move an object (usually a window, dialog box, or database) to a new position on-screen. You do this by clicking and dragging the object. To *drag* an object to a new location on-screen, point to the object, press and hold the left mouse button, move the mouse to the new location, and then release the mouse button. The object moves with the mouse pointer as you drag it.

You can point to an item—a workspace page or a database icon, for example—and click the right mouse button to display a shortcut menu. The shortcut menu usually has common commands relating to that particular item. This mouse operation is called *right-clicking*.

You also can perform certain actions, such as selecting multiple items or copying items, by performing two additional mouse operations. *Shift+click* means to press and hold the Shift key while clicking the left mouse button; *Ctrl+click* means to press and hold the Ctrl key while clicking the left mouse button. The result of either of these actions depends upon where you are in Lotus Notes.

USING THE KEYBOARD

You can use the keyboard to move around in Lotus Notes and to access many, but not all, of its features. For example, you can access menus with the keyboard, but you cannot access SmartIcons.

Shortcuts If you have a choice when working with Notes, use the mouse the majority of the time, and use the keyboard mostly for shortcuts, as described throughout this book.

To open a menu with the keyboard, press the Alt key and then press the underlined letter in the menu. For example, to open the File menu, press Alt+F. The menu drops down.

To select a command from the menu, press the underlined letter in the command. Alternatively, after you open a menu you can use the up and down arrow keys to move to a command and then press Enter to select the highlighted command. See Lesson 3 for more information about menus, commands, and dialog boxes.

Within dialog boxes, press the Tab key to move from option to option, or press Alt plus the underlined letter to select an option. Press Enter when an option is selected to activate that option. You can press Enter when a dialog box's OK button is active to accept all changes you've made and close the dialog box, or you can press the Esc key to cancel changes and close the dialog box.

Finally, you can access any window's Control menu using the keyboard. Press Alt+Spacebar to open the application's Control menu. To access the workspace page Control menu, press Alt+F to open the File menu and then use the left arrow to move to the Control menu.

Cancel a Menu To cancel a menu, press the Esc key twice.

EXITING NOTES

When you're finished with Notes, you can close the program in a couple of different ways. To close Notes, do one of the following:

- Choose File, Exit Notes.
- Double-click the application's Control-menu button.
- Click on the application's Control-menu button and choose Close from the menu.

- Press Alt+F4.
- Click the Close (X) button at the right end of the Notes title bar.

In this lesson, you learned how to start and exit Notes, how to use the mouse, and how to select commands using the keyboard. In the next lesson, you'll learn some more basic Lotus Notes concepts.

LESSON

2 Understanding Domino Concepts

In this lesson, you learn some of Domino's capabilities, ways you can use Domino in your work, and terminology that describes Domino's components and procedures.

Understanding Domino's Capabilities

Lotus Domino is a *client-server* platform that enables you to access, share, and manage information over a network. The network could consist of five or ten computers in your office building cabled together or 30,000 computers across the United States connected to each other in various ways.

A Lotus Domino network is made up of at least one server and one or more clients, or workstations. A *server* is a powerful computer set aside to communicate with other computers and supply those computers with whatever they need to complete their work. A *client* is the computer that accesses the server and uses its resources.

Resources Any shared data or hardware, such as files, printers, CD-ROM drives, and so on.

For example, a server might supply a workstation with files, programs, and backup options. In addition, a Lotus Domino server supplies each workstation with a mailbox and a place to store information that everyone can share.

You can communicate with others on the network by sending and receiving mail messages or through online group discussions.

You can collaborate with your coworkers by sharing such documents as text files, spreadsheets, graphics, and tables that you use in your work every day.

COMMUNICATING OVER THE NETWORK

Someone working at a workstation can create e-mail (electronic mail) messages, or memos, that he or she can send to anyone else on the network using Lotus Domino. The message travels across the network to the Lotus Domino server and remains in the specified mailboxes until the owners of the mailboxes open and read their mail. The recipients can then reply to the message.

Another form of communication over the network is the discussion group. A *discussion group* can consist of two or more people connected to the network. When you join a discussion group, you type messages on-screen in Lotus Notes, while others in the discussion group read your message and reply. You get immediate feedback from your messages, just as you would over the phone.

SHARING INFORMATION OVER THE NETWORK

You also can use Notes to share *documents* over the network. These might include reports, letters, or tables of data. The Domino server contains many *databases*, collections of documents you can tap into and read, or even store on your computer.

Generally, a company will use the server to store many documents that its employees may need for work (such as instructions, regulations, and guidelines). Additionally, anyone connected to the network can create a document database and add it to those on the server for you and others to access. You can even create document databases yourself and add them to those already on the server.

HOW DO YOU FIT IN?

When using Lotus Notes, you can work either on the local drive or on the network drive. When you work on the *local* drive, you are working with the files, databases, or messages stored on your computer's hard drive. When you work on the *network* drive, you are accessing files and such stored on the server. Which you choose depends on your current project.

Local versus Network The local drive refers to your workstation's hard drive (usually C). The network drive refers to a drive you connect to through the LAN (local area network) or WAN (wide area network); it might be drive F, G, or H, for example.

Lotus Domino gives you the choice of Local or Network depending on the task you're about to perform. For example, when you open a database, you must tell Domino whether the database is on your local drive or on the network.

WORKING ON LOCAL

You can choose to work on your local drive whether or not you're connected to the network. For instance, you might be at home or on the road using your laptop, in which case you're not physically connected to the network. Or you might be physically connected, but using files and databases on your hard drive instead of the network resources.

The advantages to working on local are that you get quicker data access times, you don't have to hassle with network traffic, and you can work away from the office. However, you have to use more of your hard drive's disk space, your data selections are limited, and you are unable to interact with coworkers through mail or discussion groups.

Working Alone? You can create mail while working locally and then connect to the network to send the mail. While you're connected to the network, you can also access other databases and discussion groups. (See Lesson 26 for more information on remote access to Domino.)

WORKING ON THE NETWORK

When you work on the network, you can access files, send and receive mail, or join a discussion group while attached to the network drive. You might choose the network drive so you can access certain files and then add them to your local drive for quick and easy access at any time. Or you might just want to work in the files directly on the network.

Network Access When you choose to access a database that's stored on the network drive, you can only use that database while connected to the network. If you disconnect from the network, the database is no longer available to you.

You'll find several advantages to using the network drive. First, you have access to a larger selection of data and information. In addition, you have direct mail connections with coworkers, and you can receive immediate feedback through discussion groups. Of course there are also disadvantages to using the network drive. For example, network traffic may cause slower access times, and you might run into long wait times when trying to access certain sought-after information.

UNDERSTANDING DOMINO AND NOTES TERMINOLOGY

If you're used to working on a *stand-alone* computer (one that's not attached to a network), you may want to read over this section for clarification of some terms.

As you just learned, Lotus Domino works as a client-server application. Your computer is the client that accesses the Notes server for purposes of e-mail, discussion groups, and information sharing. Depending on the type of network you're attached to, you might hear the following terms used in reference to networks and Domino in addition to those already discussed in this lesson.

Network Your workstation is attached to a network that enables you to share files, printers, and applications, as well as Lotus Domino. The network might be Windows NT, OS/2, Novell, or some other network type.

File Server Your network most likely uses at least one file server. A file server is a powerful computer that holds all data and applications shared over the network, all information about each user on the network, and so on.

System Administrator Your system administrator is the person who manages the network file servers and resources, sets passwords and securities, and troubleshoots problems with the network.

Domino Network The Domino network is an additional network set up on Windows NT, OS/2, or some other network.

Domino Server A computer specified as a server to handle Notes traffic (such as mail and databases) using specific application software from Lotus. Very large organizations may have more than one Domino server.

Domino Administrator A Domino administrator is the person who manages and organizes Notes users and Domino servers. This person sets security for Domino, troubleshoots Domino problems, and so on.

Workgroup A group of workstations on a network identified by a workgroup name. The system administrator creates and uses workgroups to make viewing and organizing workstations on the network easier.

Domain In Windows NT networks, a collection of computers, users, or workgroups gathered within a network or over several networks. Domains enable the system administrator to assign rights and permissions to a group, which is much easier than assigning them to each individual separately.

Protocol The language your computer uses to communicate over the network. The workstation must use whichever protocol the server uses. Additionally, Lotus Domino servers and clients use the same protocol as the network.

Permissions and Rights Privileges assigned to each user or workstation, thereby providing access to the server(s) and resources on the network.

User ID Every Notes user has a unique ID used to store his or her access privileges to the Domino server. You can password-protect your User ID so that no one else can use it; see your Domino administrator for more information.

Password You generally must use a password to attach, or *log on,* to any network. (The operating system usually supplies a dialog box or screen prompt when you turn your computer on.) Also, you may need a password to access certain tasks or procedures in Lotus Notes. If you are prompted to give a password and you do not know what that password is, check with your Domino administrator.

In this lesson, you learned some of the tasks you can accomplish using Domino and Notes, how Notes and you fit into a network structure, and some common networking terms you may need in order to work in Notes. In the next lesson, you'll learn to use menus, commands, InfoBoxes, dialog boxes, SmartIcons, views, and the Status bar.

Getting Started with Notes

LESSON 3

In this lesson, you learn to use Notes menus and commands, SmartIcons, workspace pages, the Status bar, and views.

Opening Menus and Selecting Commands

As do most Windows applications, Notes supplies *pull-down menus* that contain the commands you use to work in Notes. Each menu contains a list of commands that relate to the operation of Notes. For example, the Edit menu contains such commands as Cut, Copy, Paste, and Clear. In addition, some menus change depending on the task you're performing; for example, Notes adds the Actions menu to the menu bar when you open a database.

Pull-Down Menu A menu that includes a list of related commands or actions. You pull the menu down by activating it with the mouse or the keyboard.

To open a menu using the mouse, click on the menu name in the menu bar. To open a menu using the keyboard, press the Alt key, and then press the underlined letter in the menu name. (For example, to open the File menu, you can press Alt+F.) Either way, the menu drops down to display a list of related commands (see Figure 3.1).

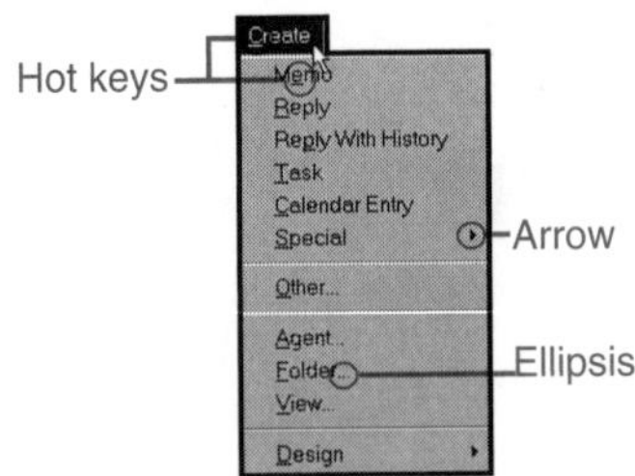

FIGURE 3.1 Pull-down menus contain the commands you use to work in Notes.

To select a command using the mouse, simply click on it. To activate a command using the keyboard, press the *hot key* of the command you want. If selecting a command leads to a secondary menu, click on a command in the secondary menu or press its hot key to activate it.

Hot Key The underlined letter in a menu name, command, or other option that you press (often in combination with the Alt key) to activate that option. Also referred to as the *accelerator key*.

Menus can contain a number of elements along with the commands. For example, some commands have hot keys you can use to access them from the keyboard, and some have keyboard shortcuts with which you can bypass the menu altogether. In addition, certain symbols may appear in a menu to give you an indication as to what will happen when you activate the command. Table 3.1 describes the command indicators you may see in a menu.

TABLE 3.1 COMMAND INDICATORS

ELEMENT	DESCRIPTION
Arrow	Indicates that another menu, called a secondary or cascading menu, will appear when you select that command.

ELEMENT	DESCRIPTION
Ellipsis	Indicates that a dialog or InfoBox will appear when you select that command.
Hot key	Marks the letter key you press to activate the menu or command using the keyboard.
Check mark	Indicates that an option or command is selected or active.
Shortcut	Provides a keyboard shortcut you can use to activate the command without accessing the menu; you cannot use the shortcut if the menu is open.
Dimmed command	Indicates that the command cannot be accessed at the current time. (For example, you cannot tell Notes to delete unless you've selected something for it to delete; so if nothing is selected, the Delete command is not available.)

Cancel a Menu To cancel a menu, point to any blank area of the workspace and click once. Alternatively, you can press the Esc key twice.

USING DIALOG BOXES AND INFOBOXES

Often, selecting a menu command causes Notes to display a dialog box or InfoBox. You can use dialog boxes and InfoBoxes to set more options and make specific choices related to the menu command. Each type of box contains certain elements you need to understand in order to use it.

DIALOG BOXES

Figure 3.2 shows the Open Database dialog box. It contains most of the elements common to Notes dialog boxes. Table 3.2 describes those elements and tells you how to use them.

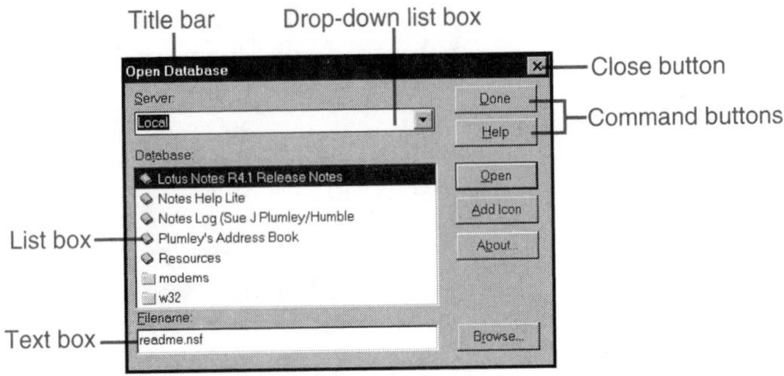

FIGURE 3.2 Use dialog boxes to make additional choices related to the selected menu command.

TABLE 3.2 DIALOG BOX ELEMENTS

ELEMENT	DESCRIPTION
Title bar	Indicates the name of the dialog box (such as the Open Database dialog box).
Drop-down list box	Displays one option from a list; click the arrow to the right of the box, and the box drops down to display the entire list.
List box	Displays a list of options so you can see more than one choice at a time.
Scroll bar	Enables you to display additional items in a window or list box; click the up or down arrow to see more.

ELEMENT	DESCRIPTION
Text box	Enables you to enter a selection by typing it in the box.
Command button	Completes the commands or leads to another related dialog box containing more options.
Close (X) button (Windows 95)	Closes the dialog box without saving changes.
Check boxes	Enable you to select or deselect options individually; when the option is selected, a check mark appears in a small square box beside the option.
Check list	Enables you to select one or more items from a displayed list of options; click an option to select or deselect it, and a check mark appears beside it or disappears (respectively).

To use a dialog box, you make your selections as described in Table 3.2, and then choose a command button. The following list describes the functions of the most common command buttons:

- *OK* or *Done* accepts and puts into effect the selections you've made in the dialog box, and then closes the dialog box.
- *Cancel* cancels the changes you've made in the dialog box and closes it (as does the Close (X) button at the right end of the title bar).
- *Browse* (or any other button with an ellipsis following the button's name) displays another dialog box.

- *Open* (or any other button with only a command on it) performs that command.
- *Help* displays information about the dialog box and its options.

I Can't Get Rid of the Dialog Box Once you've opened a dialog box, you must cancel or accept the changes you've made and close that dialog box before you can continue with your work in Notes. Use the command buttons or the Close (X) button in Windows 95 to close the dialog box.

INFOBOXES

An InfoBox also presents options related to the menu command. However, you work with an InfoBox in a different way than you do a dialog box. An InfoBox displays only the properties of a specific item, such as a workspace or a database. *Properties* are types of information about an item such as its name, location, settings, design, size, and so on. When you make a selection in an InfoBox, it takes effect immediately—even though the InfoBox remains onscreen as you work.

InfoBoxes contain *tabs* that offer various types of options about the subject. Figure 3.3 shows the Properties for Database InfoBox.

Tabs A tab in an InfoBox is similar to a tab in a drawer full of file folders. Select a tab to see information related to the tab's title.

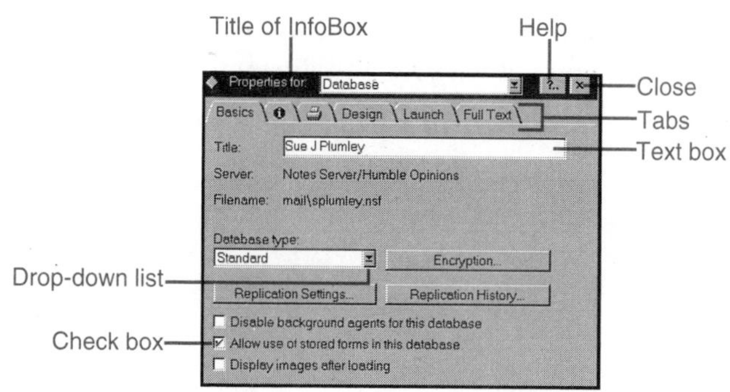

FIGURE 3.3 Use an InfoBox to change properties, or definitions, of selected items.

InfoBoxes have many of the same elements that dialog boxes have: drop-down lists, list boxes, text boxes, and check boxes, for example. However, InfoBoxes also contain the additional elements described in Table 3.3.

TABLE 3.3 INFOBOX ELEMENTS

ELEMENT	DESCRIPTION
Title of InfoBox	All InfoBox titles begin with "Properties for." You select the element for which you want to change the properties in the drop-down list in the title bar. You can change the properties of a database or a workspace.
Tabs	Named flaps that represent pages of options related to the selected element.
Help	Click the Help button and then click on any item in the InfoBox to view an explanation or definition of the item.

A Properties for InfoBox remains on-screen until you close it by clicking its Close (X) button. However, changes you make in the box take effect immediately; you don't have to okay them. If an open InfoBox is in your way, you can move it around on the screen by clicking on the title bar and dragging it to a new position.

Collapse and Expand Double-click an InfoBox's title bar to *collapse* it. Collapsing hides all but the title bar and the tabs and frees up space on the workspace. Double-click the title bar again to expand the InfoBox back to its original view and size.

Using SmartIcon Shortcuts

As do other Lotus applications, Lotus Notes includes SmartIcons you can use to perform common tasks quickly. Notes supplies specific SmartIcons depending on your task and your location in the Notes program. When in Workspace view, for example, the SmartIcons offer shortcuts for saving files, editing tasks, creating mail, and so on. On the other hand, when you're viewing an open database, the SmartIcons offer shortcuts for viewing documents and lists and for searching for specific text.

Notes includes more than 150 SmartIcons you can use as shortcuts. Notes arranges many of the icons in sets that are useful for performing specific actions, such as formatting or editing a document. To change the SmartIcon set that's displayed, choose File, Tools, SmartIcons. In Show, make sure the Context Icons check box is selected (if a check mark doesn't appear in the check box, click the option) and choose OK.

To find out what a SmartIcon represents, hold the mouse pointer over the icon, and a bubble or description appears containing the name of the menu command for which the icon is a shortcut. Figure 3.4 shows a description for the SmartIcon that represents the Create, Mail, Memo command.

To activate a SmartIcon, simply click on it. The most common SmartIcons and the commands they represent are listed on the inside front and back covers of this book.

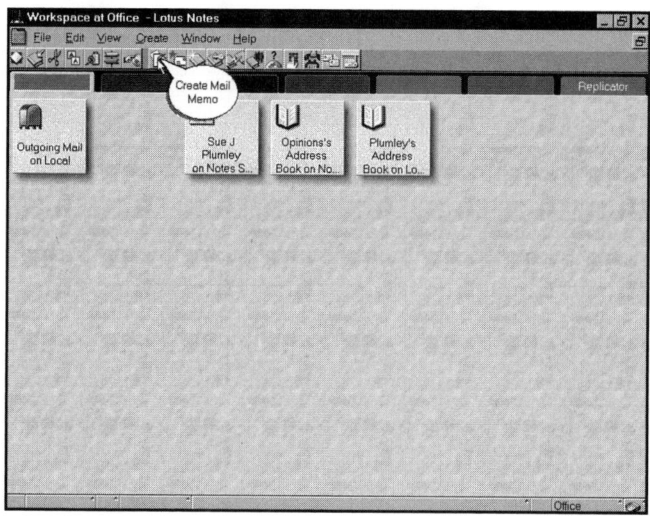

FIGURE 3.4 SmartIcon descriptions tell you what the icons do.

Modify SmartIcons You can customize SmartIcons by choosing File, Tools, SmartIcons. For more information, see Lesson 24.

USING WORKSPACE PAGES

Workspace pages are similar to file folders in that each page has a tab and an area in which you can place *databases*. Your Notes desktop contains six workspace pages, and you use the tabs to move from one page to another. To customize your workspace, you can name the tabs and organize the pages any way you want.

Database A collection of information represented by an icon on the workspace. In Notes, that information might be addresses, incoming or outgoing mail, spreadsheet documents, or word processing documents, among other things.

By default, the first page of the workspace contains items related to mail—address books and your mailbox, for example. You can move or remove these items, or you can add other items to the workspace pages.

- To move to another page in your workspace, click the page's tab.
- To move a database icon around on the displayed page, click and drag the icon. A hand appears in place of the mouse pointer, and the database icon moves with it. When you reach the desired location, release the mouse button.
- To select a database icon on the workspace page, click on the icon.

You can right-click a blank area of the workspace to display a shortcut menu of commands related to the workspace. Choose Workspace Properties from the shortcut menu to view information about the workspace. See Lesson 10 for more information about workspace pages; see Lesson 11 for more information about databases.

USING VIEWS

When you open any database, Notes displays the contents of the database in a list. This list is called a *view*. Each line in the database represents one document, person, mail message, or other item. The line gives you information about each entry, such as name, address, subject, date, or other data. No two database lists look exactly alike, and the elements displayed within the view depend upon which database you're viewing.

Explanation Pages Many databases open up to display an explanation page that gives you information about the database. For more information, see Lesson 11.

Figure 3.5 shows a mailbox view. From the mailbox, you send, receive, forward, delete, read, and answer messages (see Lesson 5). After you've opened a database to view its contents, you can return to the workspace by choosing File, Close.

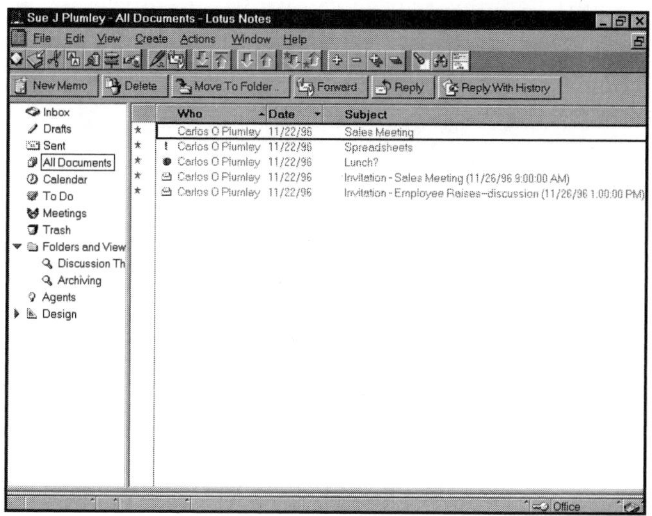

FIGURE 3.5 A view lists the various elements in the database.

GETTING INFORMATION FROM THE STATUS BAR

The *Status bar* is the bar across the bottom of the Notes window that displays messages, icons, and other information you'll use as you work in Notes. The Status bar is divided into sections. Some of those sections display messages, and others lead to a *popup box* or *popup menu*. Figure 3.6 shows the Status bar with the recent messages displayed in a popup box.

Popup Box or Menu A list of commands or items that appears when you click on certain Status bar buttons. A popup box displays such items as messages; a popup menu displays a list of selections.

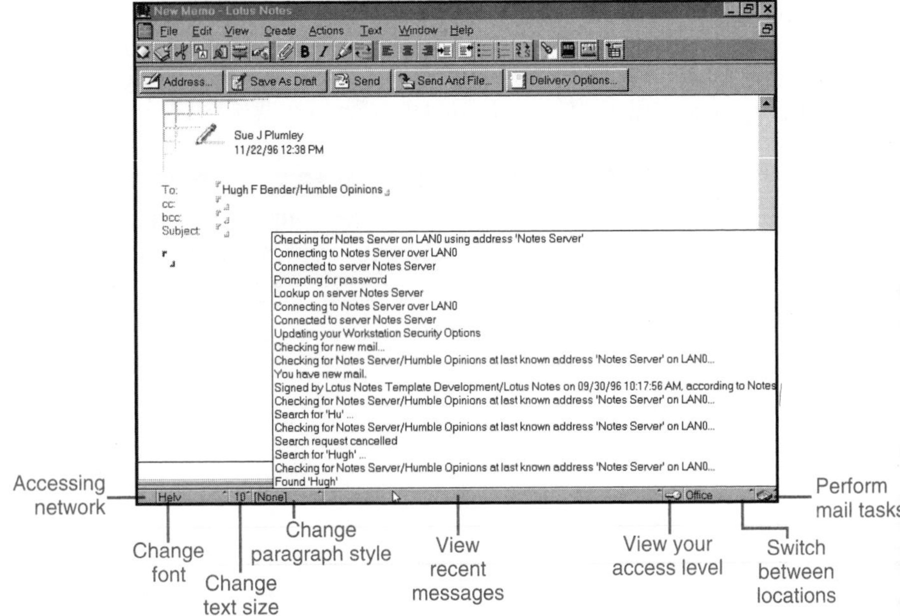

FIGURE 3.6 Use the Status bar for shortcuts and information.

As you can see in Figure 3.6, each section of the Status bar is a button with a specific function. Table 3.4 explains the Status bar buttons and their functions.

TABLE 3.4 STATUS BAR BUTTONS

BUTTON	DESCRIPTION
Accessing network	Automatically displays a lightning bolt when Notes is accessing the network; the button is blank when Notes is working from the local disk.
Change font	Displays a popup menu of fonts from which you can select a font to assign to text in a document.
Change text size	Displays a popup menu of type sizes you can assign to text in a document.

Button	Description
Change paragraph style	Displays a popup menu of paragraph styles (preformatted headings, subheads, and so on) you can apply to text in a document.
View recent messages	Displays a popup box containing messages about Notes' activities.
View your access level	Displays a dialog box that shows your status—or level of access—to open the database.
Switch between locations	Displays a popup menu that shows your current location (Office, Home, Island, or Travel) and enables you to select another.
Perform mail tasks	Displays a popup menu from which you can choose to create, send, read, and/or receive mail.

No Button Labels? If your Status bar buttons do not display labels, don't worry. Labels only appear in some of the buttons when you're in a view that (for example) uses fonts or styles. Likewise, even if the message button does not show a label, Notes always displays a list of messages when you click it.

In this lesson, you learned to use menus and commands, dialog boxes and InfoBoxes, workspace pages, and the Status bar. In the next lesson, you'll learn to use Notes' Help feature.

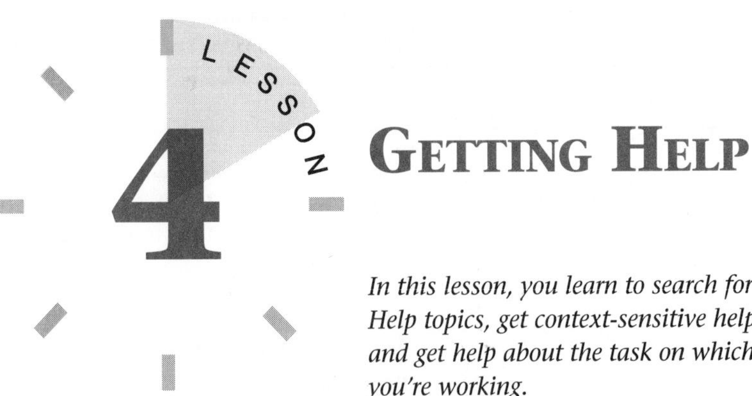

Lesson 4 Getting Help

In this lesson, you learn to search for Help topics, get context-sensitive help, and get help about the task on which you're working.

Notes provides Help from your local drive and from the server. The help you'll most likely use is that on your local drive, which is called Help Lite because it supplies quick access to information and descriptions of the most common features you'll be using in Notes. The help you access through the server, Help, contains all of Help Lite plus more advanced subjects that deal with the network, server operation, and so on. Help and Help Lite work the same.

Figure 4.1 shows the Notes Help window. The navigation pane (on the left side of the window) displays the types of help you can get, and the topics pane (on the right side of the window) shows specific topics.

The navigation pane lists the following types of help:

Contents Displays Help topics specific to common tasks and procedures, troubleshooting, and new features added to Notes.

Index Displays an alphabetical list of Help topics. Scroll through the list using the scroll bars, and select a topic by double-clicking it. In many cases, when you select a topic, more related topics appear in the list below it.

Visual Index Displays the contents of the Help database with navigators.

Search Displays an alphabetical list of phrases and words from which you can choose to view Help. If you prefer, you can also search for specific topics using the Search bar.

Printed Books Displays a list of topics found in 4.5 Guides and Books in order of their appearance in the printed book.

Favorite Topics This folder is provided so that you can easily reference frequently used help topics. You can drag and drop help documents to this folder.

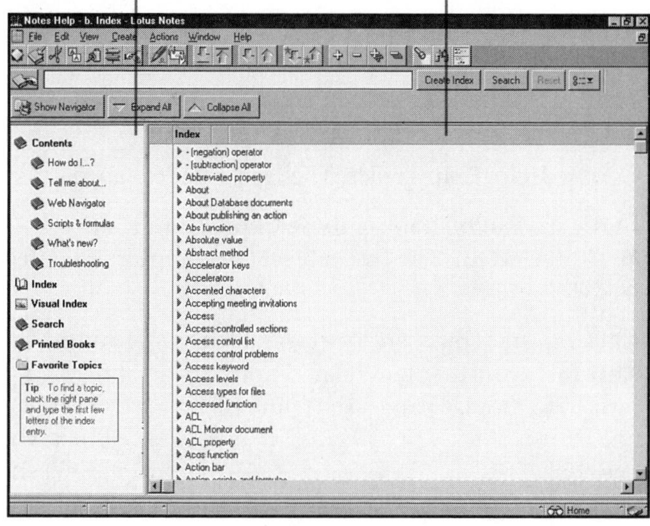

FIGURE 4.1 Choose the type of help you want.

USING CONTENTS

The Contents section lists several specific subject areas you can use when searching for tasks or procedures. The following list describes each item in the Contents list.

- **How do I?** Provides help for everyday tasks, developing and managing databases, using LotusScript, and administering Notes Server.
- **Tell me about** Provides help for shortcuts and general concepts; also gives information on functions and commands.
- **Web Navigator** Provides help in using the Personal and Server Web Navigators.

- **Scripts and formulas** Provides help for using LotusScript programming language and writing formulas. This view is designed for application developers.
- **What's new?** Displays topics related to upgrading to Release 4 and learning about the version's new features.
- **Troubleshooting** Lists common questions, error messages, release notes, and so on.

To use the Contents section of Help, follow these steps:

1. Choose Help, Help Topics. The Help window appears.
2. In the navigation pane, choose Contents (if it's not already selected). The five subject areas appear, indented below Contents.
3. Click on the subject area you want, such as **How do I** or **Tell me about**. Topics related to that type of help appear in the topics pane (see Figure 4.2).

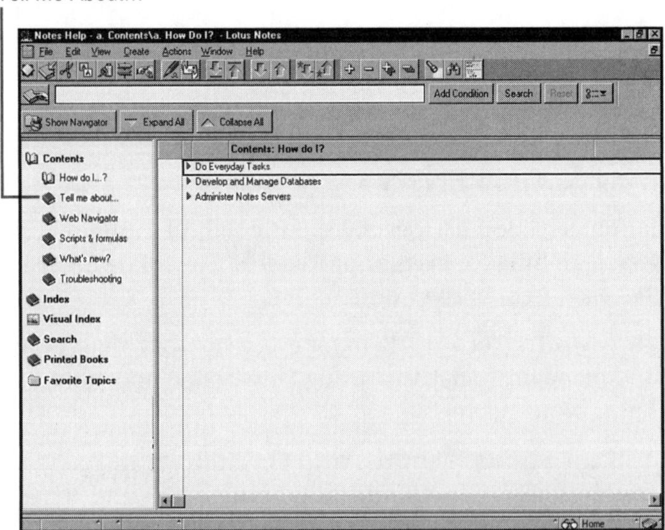

FIGURE 4.2 Select Tell Me About to display documents about Notes concepts.

4. A page icon in front of a topic means the topic represents a Help document. Double-click on any topic in the topics pane, and Notes displays the Help document. Figure 4.3 shows a typical Help document.

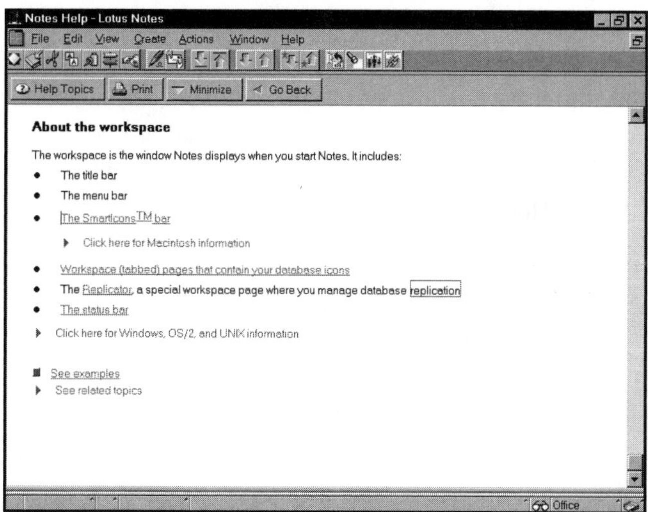

FIGURE 4.3 A Help document might contain a definition and describe how to complete a task or procedure.

5. When you're finished with the Help document, you can click on any of the following tool buttons:

Help Topics Takes you back to the list of topics and Help types.

Print Sends the displayed Help text to the printer.

Minimize Minimizes, or reduces, the Help window to an icon on the Notes desktop. You can click the icon on the desktop to open the window again.

Go Back Takes you back to the previously viewed Help screen.

> TIP **Closing Help** You can close Help at any time by choosing File, Close.

USING THE INDEX

Using the Help Index, you can view or search through an alphabetical list for tasks and topics. *Topics* are Notes features (usually nouns) such as "Databases," "Doclinks," "Files," or "Icons," whereas *tasks* are actions (verbs) such as "Inserting," "Linking," "Moving," and "Naming."

After you find the task or topic in the Notes Help window, you expand it to display related topics and/or tasks. For example, if you expand "Moving," Notes Help displays the following tasks and topics: "Among search word matches," "Around documents," "Buttons," "Data," "Database icons," "Hotspots," "Replicator entries," "Sections," and "SmartIcons." Expand any of the displayed topics or tasks to reveal specific documents describing how to perform a related task.

Figure 4.4 shows the Notes Help Index window. You can search for a topic in the Index window by scrolling through the topics or by using the Quick Search dialog box (as explained in the upcoming steps).

To use the Notes Help system's Index feature, follow these steps:

1. Choose Help, Help Topics. The Help window appears.
2. Click anywhere in the topics pane and type the first letter of the topic. The Quick Search dialog box appears.
3. Enter as many letters of the topic as necessary to narrow the search and click OK. Help jumps to the topic in the list of topics. Alternatively, you can scroll through the topics and tasks until you find the one you want.
4. To view a specific topic, double-click on it.

Right and Down Arrows A topic with a right-pointing arrow in front of it has related subjects within it; a down arrow indicates that all related topics are showing.

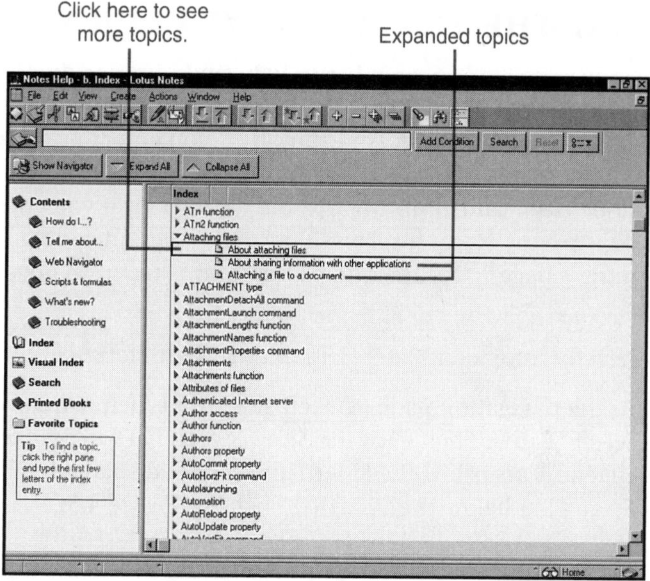

FIGURE 4.4 Look up general or specific topics using the Help Index feature.

5. Double-click the topic you want to view. (Topics you can view have a page icon next to them, representing a document.) The Help window appears, displaying the document you selected.
6. When you're finished in the Help text window, click on a tool button to return to Help Topics, print or minimize the Help document, or go back to the previous Help window.
7. When you finish using Help, choose File, Close.

Not Working? If you enter two words in the Quick Search dialog box and click OK and nothing happens, the two words are not listed together in the topics list. Try entering only the first word, and if that doesn't work, enter the second word by itself to find the topics you want.

SEARCHING FOR SPECIFIC TOPICS

You can use the Notes Search bar to help find topics and tasks. To use the Search bar, you enter a word, and Notes Help displays all topics related to that word. For example, if you enter "printing," Notes displays two related topics: "Printing a list of documents in a folder or view" and "Printing to a file." Similarly, if you enter the word "print," Notes displays 76 related topics, including "Cropping a page," "Numbering pages," and "Printing a document."

To search for a topic in Notes Help, follow these steps:

1. In the navigation pane (the left side of the Help window), select Search. Then click the Show search bar tool button that appears below the SmartIcons. Notes displays the Search bar below the SmartIcon bar (see Figure 4.5).

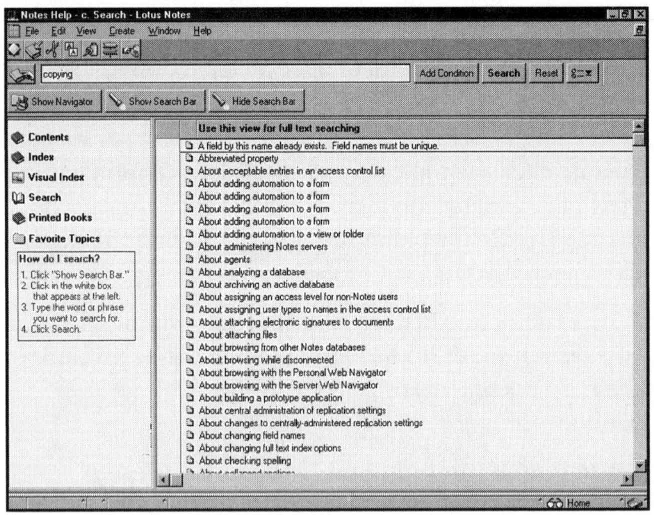

FIGURE 4.5 Search for specific topics using the Search bar.

2. Click in the Search bar text box and enter the topic—such as **print**, **copy**, **link**, or **import**—for which you want to search.

3. Click the Search button or press Enter, and Notes displays the related documents in the topics pane (as shown in Figure 4.6).

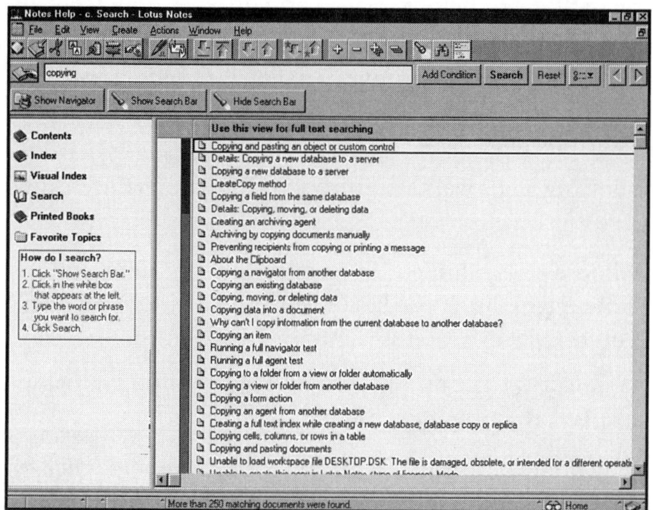

FIGURE 4.6 Notes displays related documents; double-click one to view it.

4. Double-click on the name of any document to view it.
5. (Optional) From within a Help document, click the Go Back button to return to the Notes Help window and choose another document from the displayed list.
6. To search for another topic or task, click the Reset button and enter a new word in the Search bar text box.
7. To close the Search bar, choose View, Search Bar.

USING CONTEXT-SENSITIVE HELP

One area of Notes Help includes step-by-step procedures for such common tasks as printing, finding a document, and creating documents so you can quickly and easily complete your work.

The Guide Me command on the Help menu lists the common topics that are available.

Guide Me is *context-sensitive* help, which means that Notes determines what type of help you need and displays only relevant, or context-sensitive, topics. If, for example, you're in your workspace tab when you select Guide Me, Help displays topics such as "Add a workspace page," "Delete a workspace page," and "Switch to a different workspace page."

The following steps walk you through using the handy Guide Me feature:

1. Choose Help, Guide Me or press F1 at any time, and Notes Help displays a list of topics related to whatever you're currently doing.
2. Double-click on a topic to read more about it, and Notes displays the Help document.
3. When you're finished with the Help document, click one of the buttons on the tool bar to go back, return to Help topics, print the topic, or close Help.

In this lesson, you learned to use the Contents, Index, and Search features of Notes' Help system. In the next lesson, you'll learn to open your mailbox, read your incoming mail, select messages, and view mail.

LESSON 5

Reading Incoming Mail

In this lesson, you learn to open your mailbox, select a message, read the message, answer mail, and close the message.

Opening Your Mailbox

When you have new mail, Notes displays a message in the Status bar to notify you. Your mailbox is a *database* stored on the server and accessed via the network.

Database A collection of related documents that you can access.

Your mailbox is usually on the first workspace page, and you can open it and read the mail whenever you want. To open your mailbox, follow these steps:

1. Move to the workspace page containing your mailbox by clicking the page's tab. Your mailbox appears as a box with your name and an envelope on it (see Figure 5.1).

TIP **Is It Selected?** When your mailbox is selected, it looks like the button is pressed in.

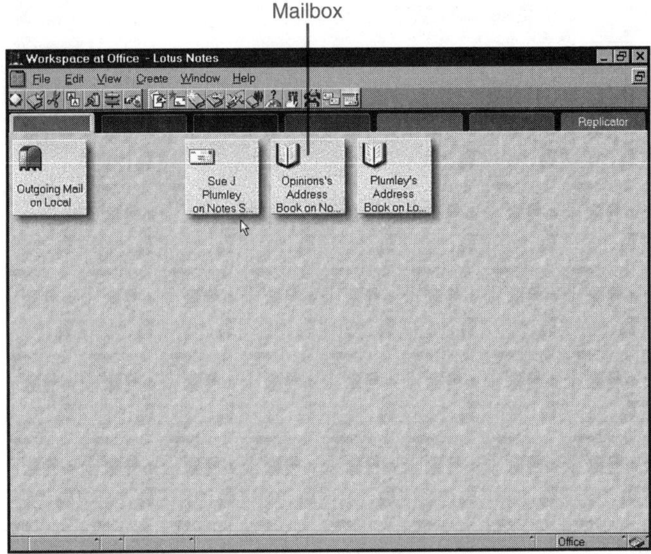

FIGURE 5.1 Your mailbox appears on the workspace.

2. Double-click on your mailbox to open it, or right-click on it and select Open from the shortcut menu that appears. An informational page set up by your Notes administrator may appear (see Figure 5.2).
3. If necessary, choose File, Close to close the informational page and display the mailbox view. Figure 5.3 shows my mailbox in the Inbox view.

No Mail? If you do not see mail, but you know you have mail waiting, click on Inbox in the navigation pane of the mailbox.

The mailbox consists of two panes and an action, or tool button, bar. The active view pane (on the right) displays your mail messages. You can see who sent the message, the date he or she sent it, and the subject he or she assigned to it.

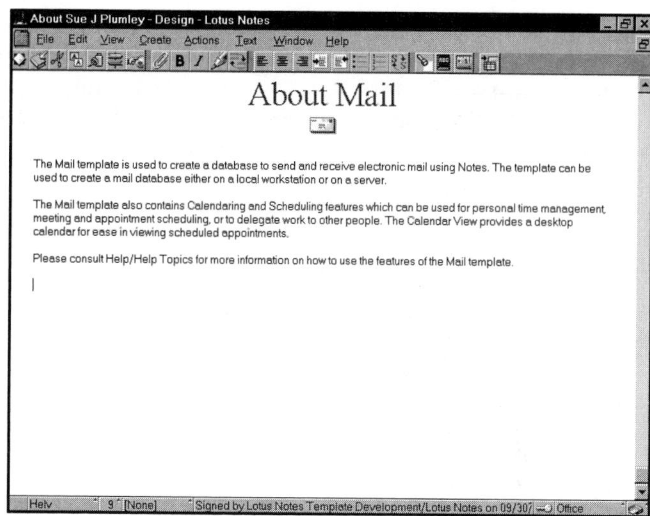

FIGURE 5.2 Many databases display an informational page.

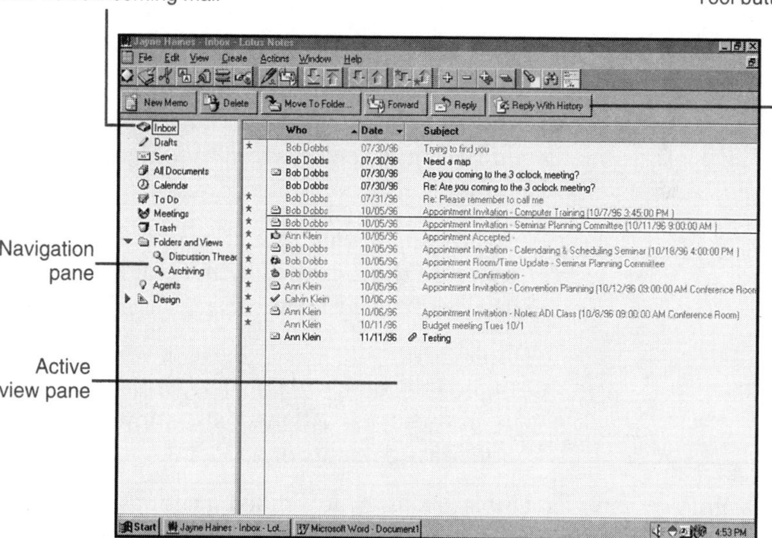

FIGURE 5.3 Notes displays your mail messages in the Inbox view.

The tool button bar contains command buttons that perform tasks related to the procedure. For example, when you're looking at your incoming messages, you can click one of these buttons to delete a message or reply to a message. The tool buttons change depending on which view you're in.

The navigation pane (on the left) lists the views you can use to manage your mail at different stages. Table 5.1 describes the views listed in the left pane of the mailbox.

TABLE 5.1 MAILBOX VIEWS

VIEW	DESCRIPTION
Inbox	Stores mail that has been sent to you.
Drafts	Stores mail messages you're working on but have not sent yet; also contains any mail you create but choose to save as a draft.
Sent	Stores copies of messages you have sent (if you choose to keep a copy of the messages).
All Documents	Displays all messages, including those you've sent, received, saved in folders, and so on.
Calendar	Displays appointments and meetings you create and those created by meeting invitations e-mailed to you.
To Do	Displays the tasks you've created, who assigned the task, the due date, and to whom the task is assigned; also shows priority assignments of 1, 2, or 3.
Meetings	Displays a list of scheduled meetings by date, time, and subject.
Trash	Holds deleted messages until you empty the trash or remove the message from the trash.

VIEW	DESCRIPTION
Folders and Views	Provides access to folders in which you can save various messages, discussions, and other important mail you receive.
Agents	Contains preset, automatic tasks such as backups and deletion of expired messages.
Design	Offers various templates for use in creating documents. (See Lesson 16 for more information.)

Down Arrows The down arrows in the navigation pane (beside Folders and Views and Design) reveal or hide additional items relating to the topic. Click the arrow to show related topics; and then click the item again to hide the topics.

SELECTING A MESSAGE

Before you can read, delete, print, or otherwise manipulate a mail message, you must first select it. One message is already selected when you open your mailbox. The selected message has a rectangle (usually black) around the name, date, and subject of the message. That rectangle functions as a *selection bar*.

To select a different message in the list, click on the message, or use the up and down arrows to move to it. To select multiple messages, press and hold the Shift key and click on the messages. A check mark appears to the left of each selected message.

READING YOUR MAIL

You can select any message in your Inbox to read at any time. To read a mail message, double-click on the message, or right-click on it and choose Open from the shortcut menu. Figure 5.4 shows an open mail message.

Every mail message, or memo, contains the following elements:

- **Heading** The heading includes the name of the person who sent the message, and the date and time he or she sent it. In addition, if you're on a Windows NT network, you may see the domain name, company name, or other information, beside the sender's name.

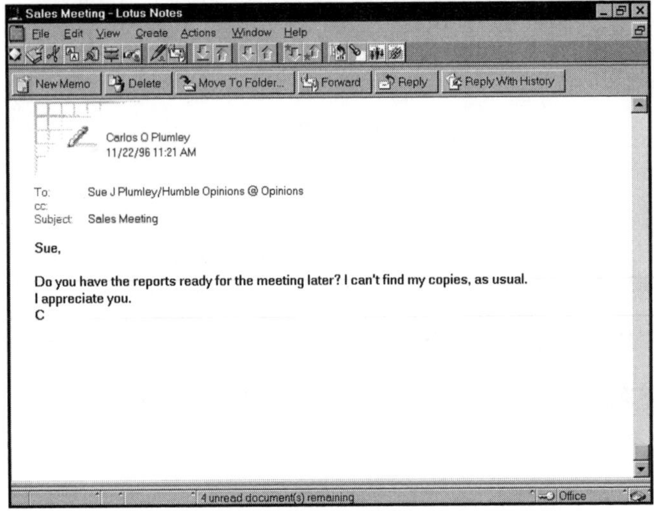

FIGURE 5.4 The open message fills the workspace.

- **To** The To line shows the name of the person to whom the message is being sent. Again, the domain name may be included.
- **cc** The cc (carbon copy) line displays a list of any others who received a copy of the message.
- **Subject** The subject describes the topic of the message, as defined by the sender of the message.

The rest of the message is the body, which is made up mostly of text but can also contain graphics (pictures), tables, and other items. A message can be as short as a word or two, or as long as 21,000 paragraphs. The length of the message is limited, of course, by your computer's memory. If you cannot view all of a message on-screen at once, use the vertical scroll bar or the Page Up, Page Down, and arrow keys to view more of the message.

Shortcuts You can press Ctrl+End to go to the end of a long message or Ctrl+Home to go to the beginning of a message.

ANSWERING MAIL

After you've read your mail, you can choose from various options. Often, you will want to reply to your mail message. To reply to a mail message, follow these steps:

1. With the mail message open, click the Reply tool button. The New Reply window appears (see Figure 5.5).

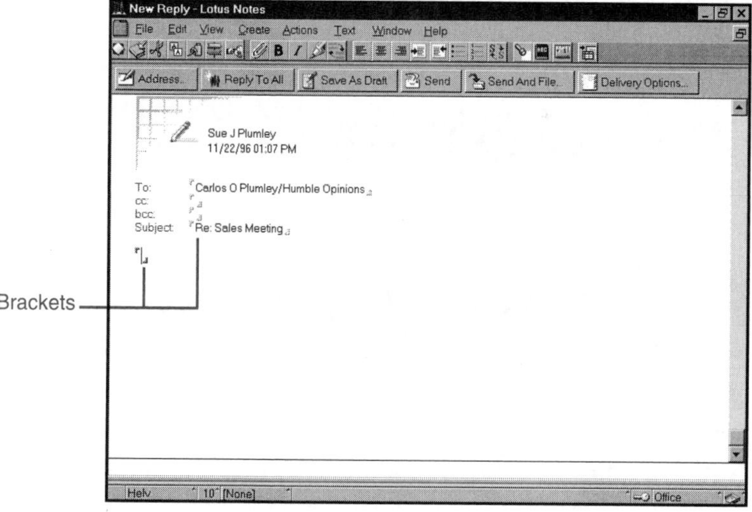

FIGURE 5.5 Notes fills in the recipient's name and address.

2. To send a carbon copy of the message to another party, click between the brackets after **cc** and enter the name(s).

To send a blind carbon copy, enter the name of the party in the brackets after **bcc**. (A blind carbon copy is sent to someone without the primary recipient knowing it.)

3. Position the insertion point between the brackets in the message body and begin typing the message.
4. (Optional) Click the Reply With History tool button to have Notes attach a copy of the original message to the reply.
5. When you're ready, click the Send button to send your reply. For more information about creating and sending your own mail, see Lesson 7.

CLOSING A MESSAGE AND THE MAILBOX

When you reply to or forward a message, Notes closes the message automatically when you select Send (however, you still have to close the original message). If you choose not to reply to the message at this time, you must close it to return to the mailbox.

To close the message without performing any additional tasks, choose File, Close. Notes returns to the mailbox, and you can read other messages or exit the mailbox. To exit the mailbox, choose File, Close.

Delete the Message If you're sure you do not need the message, click the Delete tool button to delete it.

In this lesson, you learned to open and close your mailbox and work with your mail messages displayed there. In the next lesson, you'll learn to manage mail from the mailbox view while performing such tasks as printing and deleting messages and saving messages in a folder.

Managing Incoming Mail

LESSON 6

In this lesson, you learn to print, delete, and forward messages, and to save a message to a folder.

Printing Mail

When you're viewing your mail in the Inbox, you can perform a variety of tasks on selected mail using the commands on the shortcut menu. For example, you can print a message without opening it. To print a mail message, follow these steps:

1. In the Inbox, select the message you want to print and right-click on the message. The shortcut menu appears (see Figure 6.1).

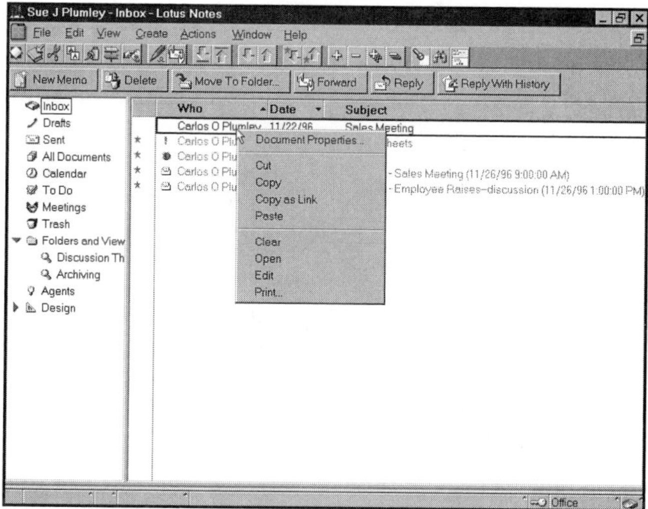

Figure 6.1 Use the shortcut menu to print a message from the Inbox.

2. Choose the Print command, and the File Print dialog box shown in Figure 6.2 appears. Table 6.1 describes this dialog box's options in detail.

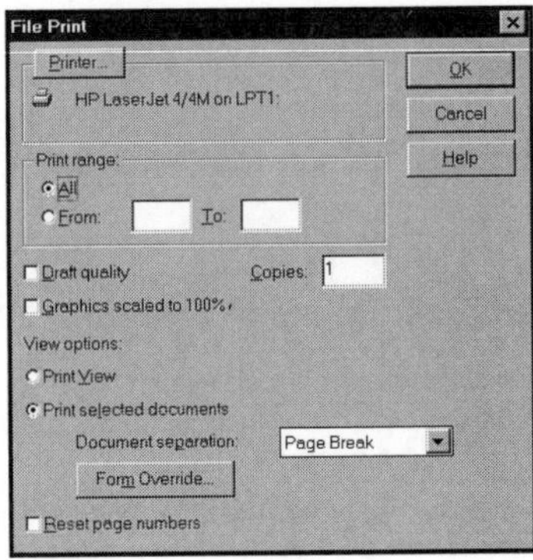

FIGURE 6.2 Set print options in the File Print dialog box.

3. Set the print options to meet your needs (see Table 6.1), and then click OK to print the message.

TABLE 6.1 COMMON PRINTING OPTIONS

OPTION	DESCRIPTION
Printer	Select this button if the printer listed in the box is not the correct one. In the Print Setup dialog box that appears, choose the printer you want to use.
Print range	Select All to print all pages of the message, or select From and To and enter the page numbers for the range you want to print in the text boxes.

OPTION	DESCRIPTION
Draft quality	Select this option if you don't need a letter-quality copy (dark text and nice-looking graphics). Draft quality enables the printer to print more quickly.
Graphics scaled to 100%	Select this option if there are pictures in the message and you want them to appear full-sized on the printout.
Copies	Enter the number of copies of the message you want to print.
Print View	Select this option to print a copy of the Inbox view with a list of your messages.
Print selected documents	Choose this option to print the selected message(s) in the Inbox view.

Print Multiple Messages You can print two or more messages at the same time by holding the Shift key while clicking on each message; a check mark appears to the left of the selected messages. Then right-click any selected message and choose Print. Finally, in the File Print dialog box, make sure you select the Print Selected Documents option.

DELETING MAIL

You can delete one or more messages in the Inbox by selecting the messages and marking them for deletion. A message marked for deletion remains in the Inbox until you empty the trash or until you exit the Notes program. The following steps walk you through deleting a message, in case you don't want to wait until you exit Notes:

1. Select the message(s) you want to delete and click the Delete tool button. When you click the Delete tool button, a trash can icon appears to the left of the selected message, marking that message for the trash.

2. To empty the trash, click Trash in the navigation pane. You'll see the message you marked for deletion in the view pane as shown in Figure 6.3.

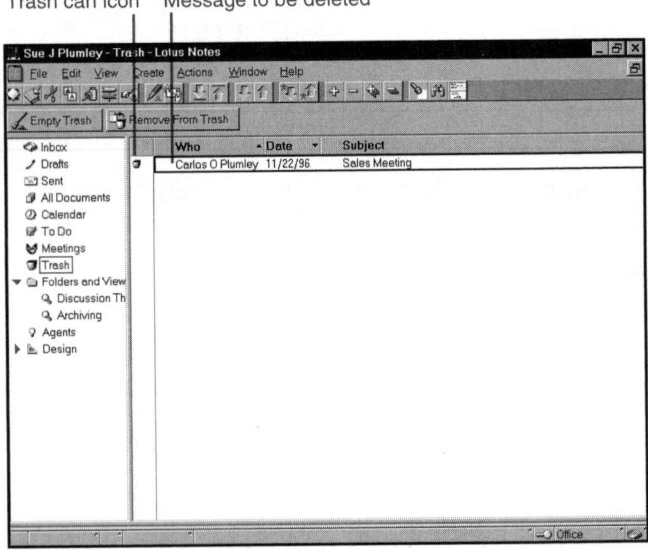

FIGURE 6.3 Message marked for deletion in Trash view.

3. To delete the message, click the Empty Trash tool button. A confirmation message appears; click Yes to delete the message.

4. To return to the Inbox, click Inbox on the left side of the mailbox pane.

Change Your Mind? If you decide you don't want to delete a message shown in Trash view, select it and click the Remove From Trash tool button.

SAVING MAIL IN A FOLDER

If you want to save a mail message, you can assign it to an existing folder. (However, you cannot save messages to the Folders and Views folder in the navigation pane.) If you don't like the choice of existing folders, you can create your own folders in which to save your mail. To save mail in a folder, follow these steps:

1. In the Inbox, select the mail message you want to save.
2. Click the Move To Folder tool button. The Move To Folder dialog box appears.
3. Select Folders and Views and then click the Create New Folder button.
4. In the Create Folder dialog box that appears, enter a name for the new folder and click OK. Notes closes the Create Folder dialog box and returns to the Move To Folder dialog box, which now includes the name of the new folder.
5. Select the new folder and click the Move button. The dialog box closes, and Notes moves the message to the newly created folder.

New Folder The newly added folder immediately appears in the navigation pane under Folders and Views. You can open it at any time by clicking on it; its contents appear in the view pane (on the right side of the window).

FORWARDING MAIL

You can forward any mail message to another party, and you can even add your own comments or reply to it. To pass a message on to someone else, you click the Forward Mail button. The New Memo window appears (see Figure 6.4).

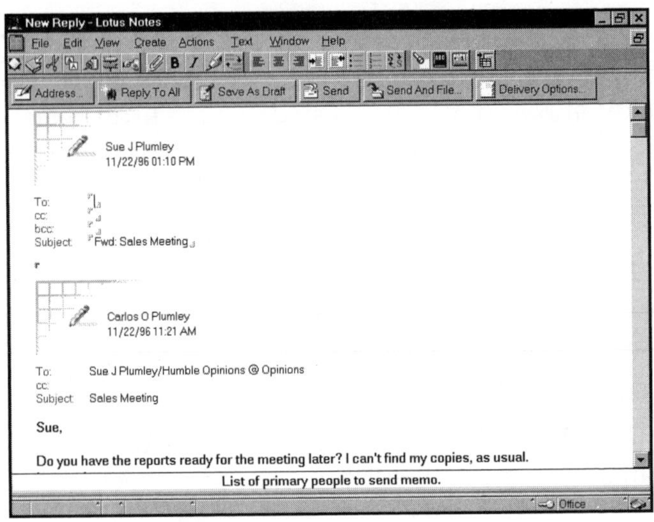

FIGURE 6.4 You can forward the message to another party and add your own comments.

The existing message moves down on the page to make room for the forwarding information. Enter the party's name and any other information you want. Then add your comments above the **Forwarded by** line and the horizontal blank line. Click the Send tool button to send the message.

In this lesson, you learned to print, delete, and forward mail, as well as to save mail in a folder for future reference. In the next lesson, you'll learn to create, address, and send your own mail messages.

LESSON 7

Creating and Sending Mail

In this lesson, you learn to create mail, address mail, and send your mail messages.

Creating Mail

The most common type of mail message is the memo. Even though the message looks like a memo (it includes To, CC, and Subject lines), you are not limited in terms of the length of the mail message or the items you can include in a mail message. (For more information on mail, see Lessons 5 and 6.)

Open your mailbox, and then follow these steps to create a mail message.

1. In your mailbox database, choose the New Memo tool button. A blank memo like the one in Figure 7.1 appears. Notes automatically fills in your name, the date, and the time.

Quick Memo You can quickly create a memo from your workspace by choosing the Create, Memo menu command. Create the memo and click Send, and Notes returns to the workspace.

2. Click in the **To** brackets and enter the name(s) of the person(s) to whom you want to send the memo. As you type a name, Notes searches your company's address book and your personal address book for the letters you've typed. If it finds a match, Notes fills in the name for you.

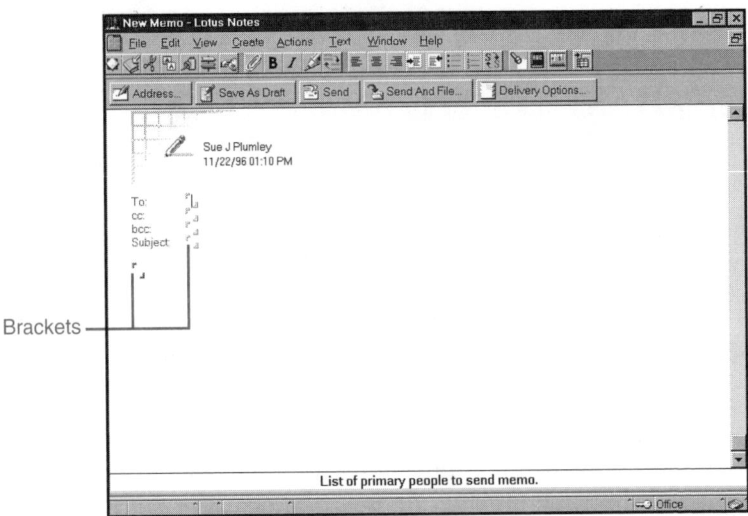

FIGURE 7.1 You start out with a blank memo.

3. (Optional) Click in the **cc** (carbon copy) brackets or press the Tab key, and then enter the name(s) of the person(s) to whom you want to send a copy of the message. Again, Notes fills in names for you if it finds the first letters you enter in either address book.
4. (Optional) Click in the **bcc** brackets and enter the name(s) of the person(s) to whom you want to send a blind carbon copy.
5. In the **Subject** brackets, enter a word or phrase to use as a title for your message.
6. In the brackets below the **Subject** line, enter the message you want to send. When entering the message, follow these guidelines:

   Press Enter only when you want to start a new paragraph.

   Use the Delete and Backspace keys to edit text as you type.

Address Book Notes provides address books you can use when sending mail. Your company's address book is stored on the Domino server and contains the names of all those people attached to the network to whom you can send messages. See the section "Using the Address Book" later in this lesson for details.

When creating a message, you can use the mailbox's SmartIcons or menu commands to add emphasis to and change the format of text in your memo. (To brush up on using SmartIcons, flip back to Lesson 3.) For example, try some of these ideas, using either the appropriate menu commands or the SmartIcons pictured:

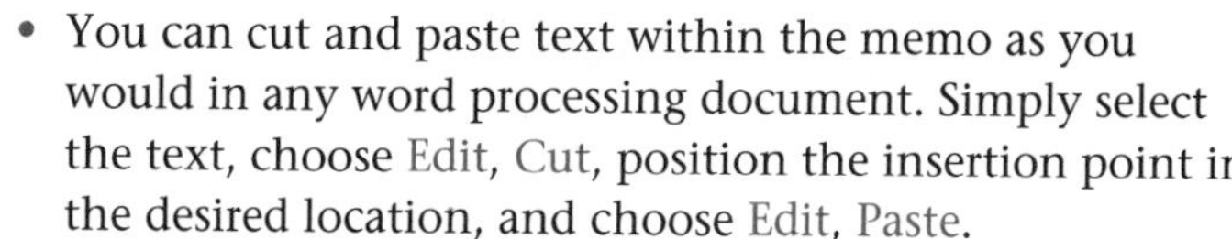

- You can cut and paste text within the memo as you would in any word processing document. Simply select the text, choose Edit, Cut, position the insertion point in the desired location, and choose Edit, Paste.

- Select any text you want to emphasize and click the Bold SmartIcon or the Italic SmartIcon. (You'll learn more about formatting text in Lesson 18.)

- Print the memo by choosing File, Print and selecting the appropriate options in the File Print dialog box (see Lesson 6 for more information).

- Check the spelling by choosing Edit, Check Spelling. (Lesson 21 covers the details of using the Spell Checker.)

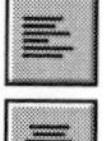

- Align selected text by clicking one of the Text Align SmartIcons. (If you're not sure which SmartIcon is which, use the Help description bubbles that you learned about in Lesson 3.)

- Indent selected text by clicking one of the Text Indent SmartIcons. (Again, if you're not sure which SmartIcon is which, use the Help description bubbles.)

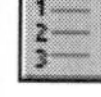

- Change a list into a bulleted list or a numbered list (respectively) by selecting the text and clicking the appropriate SmartIcon.

Selecting Text Before you can delete, format, or otherwise manipulate text, you must select it. To do so, place the insertion point to the left of the text you want to select. Then click and drag the mouse over the text to be included, and the text becomes highlighted.

SENDING MAIL

When you finish creating your mail message and are ready to send it, you can simply click the Send tool button. Notes sends the mail to the recipient's mailbox. By default, Notes saves a copy of your message in the Sent view.

To send mail and file a copy, follow these steps:

1. Choose the Send And File tool button, and the Folders dialog box appears (see Figure 7.2). From here, you can file the message in an existing folder (proceed to step 2), or you can create a new folder (skip down to step 3). However, you cannot store the message in the Folders and Views entry.

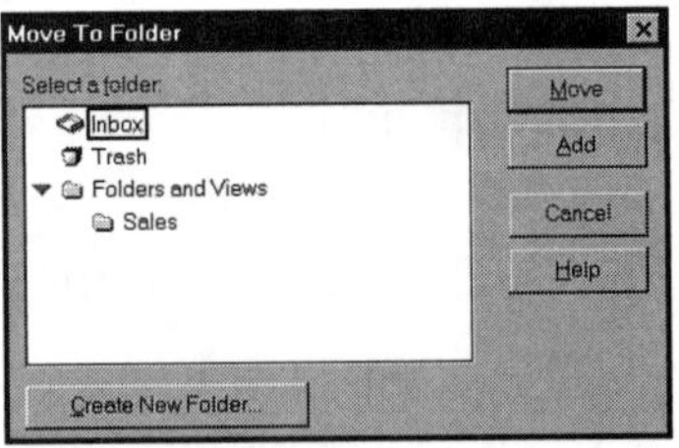

FIGURE 7.2 Save your messages in a folder for future reference.

2. To store the message in an existing folder, select the folder from the list and click OK. Notes saves the message to that folder, and you're done.
3. To create a folder, click the Create New Folder button. The Create Folder dialog box shown in Figure 7.3 appears.

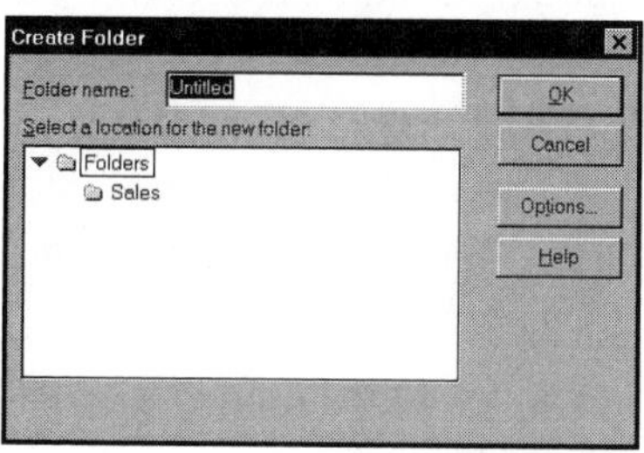

FIGURE 7.3 Select a location and enter a name for the new folder.

4. In the Folder name text box, enter a name for the new folder.
5. In the Select a location for the new folder list, choose the folder in which you want to place the new folder.
6. Click OK. Notes creates the folder and adds it to the Folders list in the Folders dialog box.
7. Select the newly created folder and click OK to store the mail message. Notes returns to the mailbox or workspace.

Two Folders Selected? If you accidentally select two or more folders in the Folders dialog box, click on any selected folder to deselect it. If Notes prompts you for a password, enter your password to complete the procedure. (If you do not know the appropriate password, see your Notes administrator.)

USING THE ADDRESS BOOK

Your Domino administrator most likely keeps up a company address book that you can use to quickly and easily find and address your mail. You may also have your own personal address book you can use. Address books usually appear on the first workspace page. Like your mailbox, the address book is a button with an icon, but its icon has a picture of an open book. The following steps teach you how to use the address book.

1. Open a new memo by clicking the New Memo tool button. Notes displays a blank memo with your personal heading.
2. Click the Address tool button, and the Mail Address dialog box appears (see Figure 7.4).

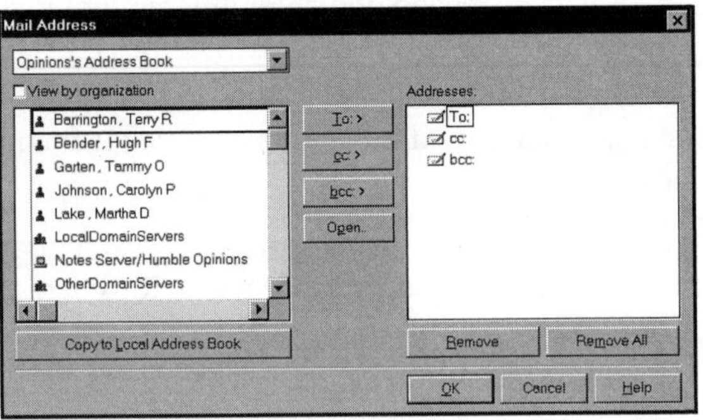

FIGURE 7.4 Use the address book to see who's available in your company or domain.

3. Open the drop-down list in the upper-left corner and choose the address book you want to look through (your company's address book, your personal book, or another domain's book, for example). Which books appear in the list depends on how your Domino administrator configured your mailbox.

4. In the list of addresses, select one recipient by clicking on his or her name. To select multiple recipients, click to the left of the desired names to display a check mark.
5. After selecting the recipient(s), choose one of the following buttons:

   To Addresses the message to the selected recipients.

   cc Sends a carbon copy to each selected recipient.

   bcc Sends a blind carbon copy to each selected recipient.

6. Click OK to close the dialog box. Notes lists the selected names in the memo. Complete the memo, and then send it or send and file it.

TIP **More Information?** To find out more information about a selected name in the address list, click the Open button. Notes displays a list of information about the person, such as his or her work title, department, and office phone number (and perhaps even the person's home address and phone number). The Notes administrator determines which additional information is included. Click Close to return to the Mail Address dialog box.

In this lesson, you learned to send mail, file your mail for future reference, and use the address book. In the next lesson, you'll learn to change mail options.

LESSON 8

Setting Mail Options

In this lesson, you learn how to choose various delivery options, as well as how to change the type of mail message you're sending.

Choosing Delivery Options

Notes lets you control the details of how and when it delivers your mail messages. You can choose delivery options to request a delivery report or to set a priority level for your mail, for example. You must set delivery options before you send your mail message. Table 8.1 describes the available delivery options.

Table 8.1 Delivery Options

Option	Description
Importance	Tags the message with an importance level (Normal, High, or Low) that the recipient can see.
Mood stamp	Provides additional messages you can add to your memo. Select a mood, and Notes adds a graphic and/or text (such as "Thank You," "Good Job," "FYI," or "Joke") to your memo.
Delivery report	Tells Notes to place a report in your mailbox that indicates how the delivery of your message went. You can have Notes confirm the delivery, trace the path of the delivery, report only on failure of the delivery, or not report at all.
Delivery priority	Marks the message as Normal, High, or Low priority. Priority governs how quickly the mail is delivered across the network.

OPTION	DESCRIPTION
Sign	Adds a unique code to your message that identifies you as the sender.
Encrypt	Encodes the message so that no one but the intended recipient can read it.
Return receipt	Places a receipt in your mailbox that tells you the time and date the recipient received the message.
Prevent copying	Prevents the recipient from copying your message.

To set delivery options, follow these steps:

1. In your mailbox, open and create a new memo. Then click the Delivery Options tool button. The Delivery Options dialog box appears (see Figure 8.1).

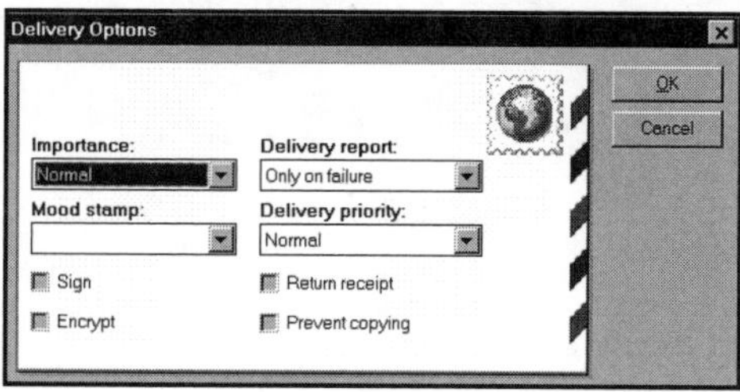

FIGURE 8.1 You control how and when your mail is delivered.

2. Open the Importance, Mood stamp, Delivery report, and Delivery priority drop-down list boxes and make your selection for each option. (Refer to Table 8.1 for details.)
3. Select or deselect the Sign, Encrypt, Return receipt, and Prevent copying check boxes as necessary. (These options are also described in Table 8.1.)
4. Click OK to set the delivery options. Then send your memo as usual.

SENDING OTHER MAIL TYPES

The most common type of mail message is the memo, but you can send other types of mail as well. For example, you can send invitations for meetings, you can send phone messages, and you can even send task assignments. The difference between the mail types is the format of the message.

SENDING A PHONE MESSAGE

The phone message memo offers an easy, timesaving method of sending someone his or her phone messages. If, for example, you take a colleague's messages while she's out of the office or in a meeting, you can enter them in Notes as you take them and then send them to her via mail. To send a phone message, follow these steps:

1. In your mailbox, choose Create, Special, Phone Message. The phone message memo appears (see Figure 8.2).

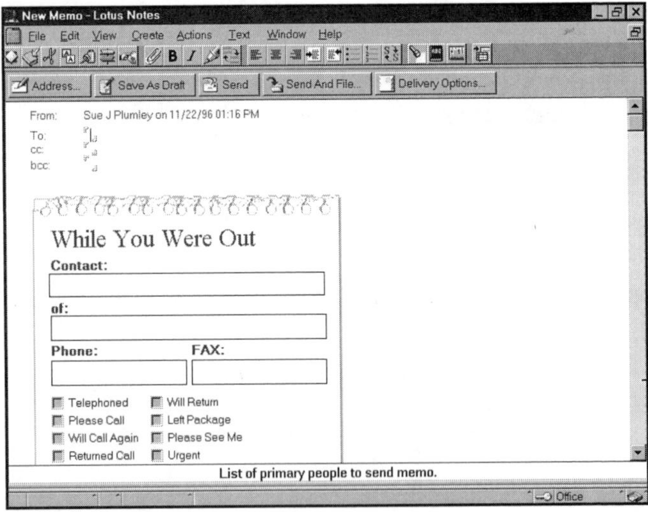

FIGURE 8.2 Take a phone message in Notes and send the person a mail message memo.

2. Enter the heading information as usual. Type the phone message information in the text boxes.

3. Send the phone message as you would any mail message.

ASSIGNING A TASK

Tasks are similar to items you place on a To Do list. You can create a task list to display in your To Do view (shown in Figure 8.3). To help you keep track of your task list, Notes enables you to choose a task, and then update it, delete it, or mark it as completed using the tool bar buttons in To Do view.

You also can choose to assign tasks to others in your organization. To assign a task, follow these steps:

1. In your mailbox, choose Create, Task. The Task memo appears (see Figure 8.4).

2. Enter a subject in the Task text box, and enter a date and priority, if you want.

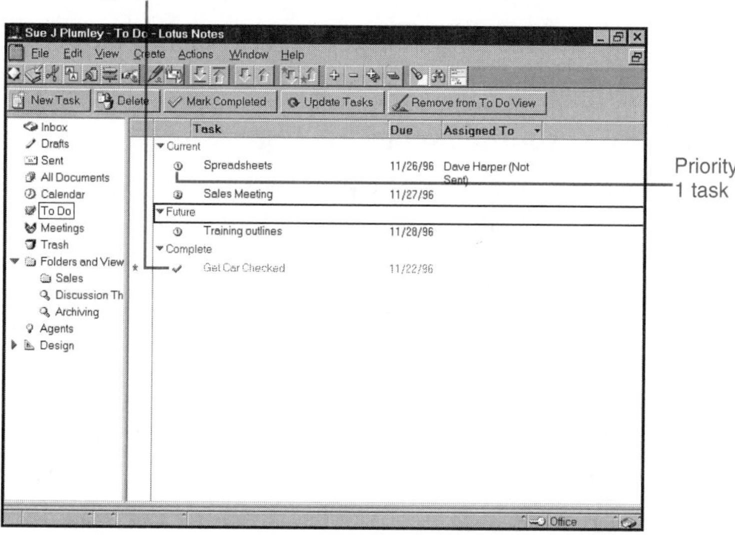

FIGURE 8.3 Use Notes' Task List to organize your duties.

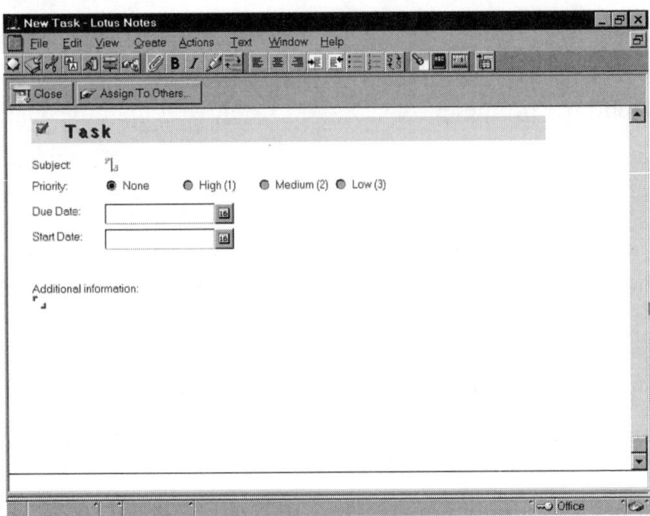

FIGURE 8.4 Assign a task to yourself or to others.

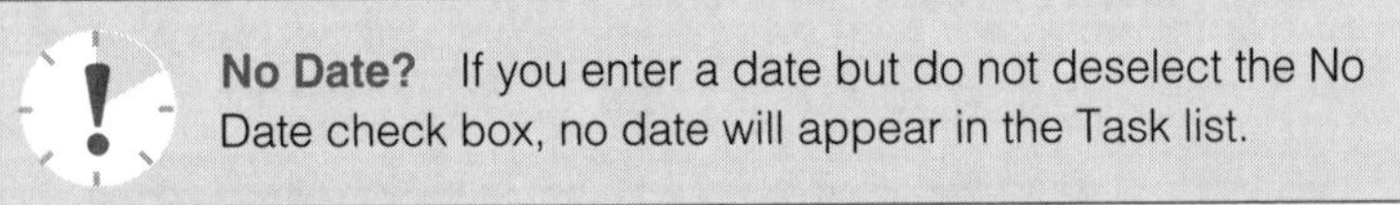

No Date? If you enter a date but do not deselect the No Date check box, no date will appear in the Task list.

3. (Optional) Enter a description of the task in the brackets below **Additional information**.
4. To assign the task to your own task list, click the Assign Now tool button. Notes adds the task to your list and returns to your mailbox in To Do view. The first time you assign a task to your own task list, a message appears telling you the task was saved in your To Do view.
5. To assign the task to someone else, click the Assign To Others tool button. The Assign To and CC *fields* appear below the Task Request graphic, and the tool bar buttons change to Address, Assign Now, and Delivery Options.

   To have the task appear in your calendar, click the Display Task On My Calendar button.

Fields In a memo or other mail message, the areas with brackets that you fill in are called "fields." Some fields, such as the To field, contain certain instructions from Notes that help you fill the field. For more information about fields, see Lesson 17.

6. Complete the message, and then send it by clicking the Assign Now tool button.

In this lesson, you learned to set delivery options and to create an invitation, a phone message, and a task. In the next lesson, you'll learn such advanced mail tasks as attaching and importing files.

LESSON 9

Using Advanced Mail Features

In this lesson, you learn to organize your mail, attach a file to a mail message, and import and export files using mail.

Organizing Mail

When working with Notes, you might be inclined to accumulate messages that you want to keep as reminders. However, accumulated messages take up valuable disk space and make it hard for you to find important items in your mailbox. To help you keep your mailbox cleaned up and to optimize your hard disk space, Notes offers these areas, or views, in which you can organize and store your messages.

- **Inbox, Drafts, Sent, and All Documents** Use these views to store both incoming and outgoing mail. For more information, see Lesson 5.
- **Trash** Place mail messages you no longer want to keep in the Trash view and then delete them from your hard disk by emptying the trash (see Lesson 6).
- **Folders** Create your own folders in which to store messages you need to keep. For example, you might create a general Sales folder, and create a folder within it for each product or service you sell. Then you can place mail messages about each product or service in their own folders so you can quickly and easily find them. (See Lesson 6 for details.)

Figure 9.1 shows the open mailbox, with the previously described views listed in the navigation pane.

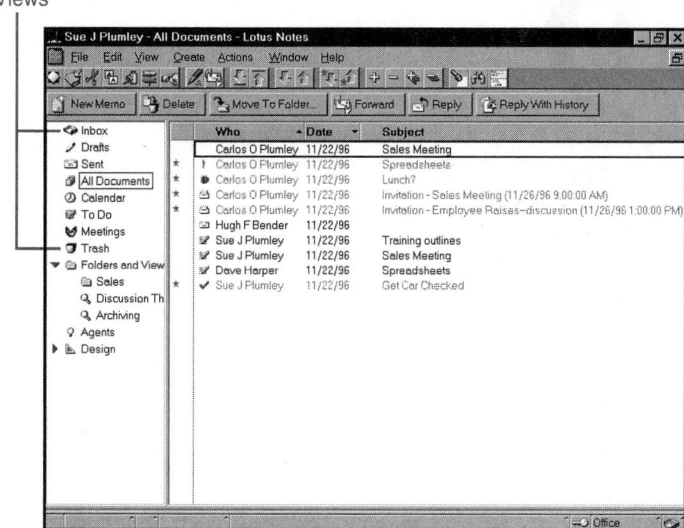

FIGURE 9.1 Use the views in the Notes mailbox to organize your mail.

Storing mail messages in certain places makes it easier for you to locate them. In addition to doing that, follow these guidelines to prevent excess files from accumulating on your hard disk. Overall, these practices conserve disk space and make managing and organizing those files you keep easier and more efficient.

- When you receive a message, deal with it immediately. You might want to delete the message after you read it, reply to the message and then delete it, or store the message in a permanent place.
- Don't save copies of the messages you send unless you really need the information in the message. Saved outgoing messages take up disk space too.
- If you must save outgoing messages, you might consider saving a printed copy instead of the copy on disk.

- Every month or so, review the messages in the Inbox, Sent, Drafts, and other views of the mailbox, and delete any messages you no longer need.

ATTACHING FILES

You can send, or attach, files—word processing documents, spreadsheets, programs, data files, and so on—with a mail message to anyone on the Notes network. To attach a file to a message, follow these steps:

1. In your mailbox, create a new memo as described in Lesson 7. Enter the addressing information and any message you want to send.
2. With your insertion point within the body text brackets, choose File, Attach. The Create Attachment(s) dialog box appears (see Figure 9.2).

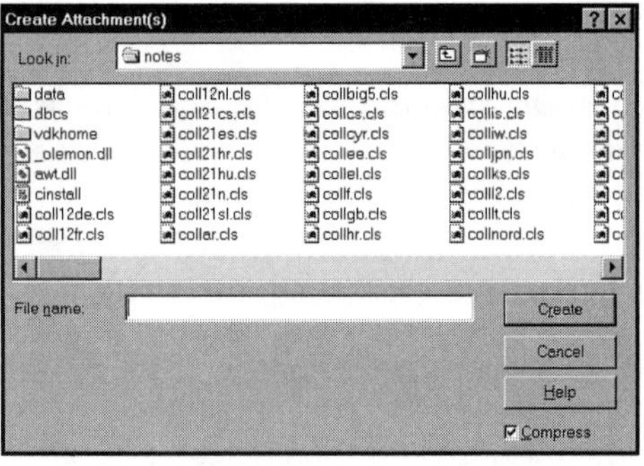

FIGURE 9.2 Choose the file you want to attach to a mail message.

3. In the Look in drop-down list, select the drive and directory containing the file you want to attach. (You can attach any file from your local drive, from a floppy drive, or from the network drive.)
4. Select the file from the list, or type the file name in the File name text box.

5. (Optional) Choose the Compress check box if you want Notes to compress the file.

Compress the File? If you choose to compress the attached file, the file is packed, or reduced in size, to speed up the transfer over the network. The recipient of the compressed file won't know the difference; Notes decompresses the file automatically when the recipient opens it.

6. Choose Create. An icon representing the file and the file's name appears in your memo (see Figure 9.3).
7. When you're finished with the message, send it as you normally would.

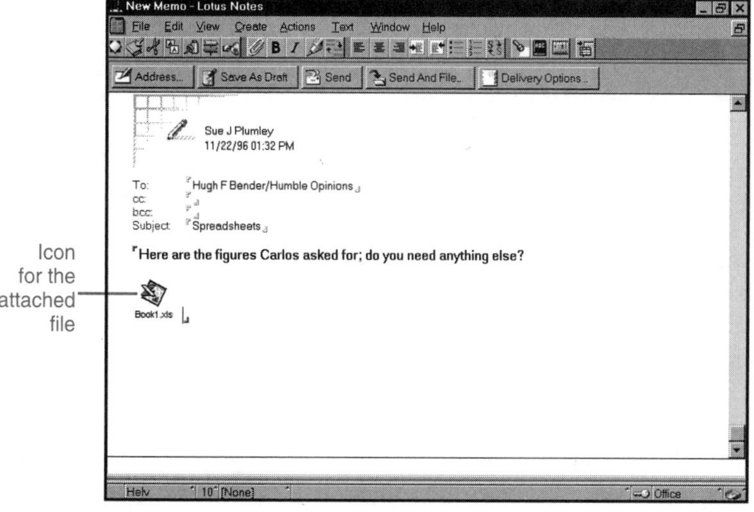

FIGURE 9.3 Attach one or multiple files to a memo, invitation, or other mail message.

In the mailbox, mail messages that contain attached files have a paper clip beside their subjects. Open such a message as you would any other, and you see that it contains an icon for the attached file. To read an attached file, double-click the file's icon. The Properties for Attachment InfoBox appears (see Figure 9.4). Click on the Information tab—with the lowercase i on it—and click one of the buttons described in the following list.

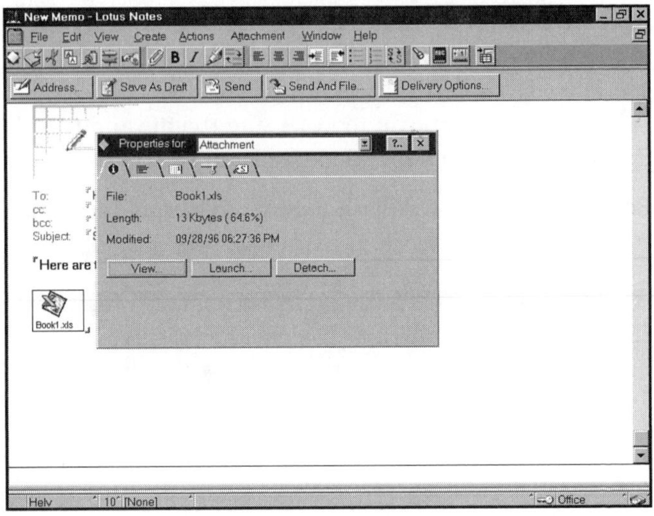

FIGURE 9.4 Use the InfoBox to control the attached file's properties.

- **View** Select this button to display the file in the File Viewer. The File Viewer does not enable you to edit the document in any way, and you can't view all file types. View may try to launch the program associated with the file type, or it may display an error. Choose File, Close to exit the File Viewer and return to the memo in Notes.
- **Launch** Choose this button to *launch*, or start, the program with which the file was created. You can edit, format, or otherwise manipulate the file using this option. Click the application's Close button to return to Notes.

- **Detach** Choose Detach to display the Save Attachment dialog box, where you choose a folder in which to store the file. You can save the file on your local drive or on the network drive, and you can save the file with the same name or a new name. Click the Detach button in the Save Attachment dialog box to complete the process.

Launch To start, or execute, a program. When you open Notes, for example, you're launching the program.

To close the InfoBox, click the Close (X) button; to open an InfoBox, right-click the attached file's icon and select Attachment Properties. To learn more about InfoBoxes, see Lesson 3. To learn more about the other tabs in the InfoBox, see Lesson 18.

Don't Worry If you want to get rid of an attached file, click on its icon and then press the Delete key.

IMPORTING FILES

You *import* a file by opening another application's file in Notes. When you do, the imported file becomes a part of Notes, taking on all characteristics and formatting of the Notes document. You might import a file if your reader doesn't have the necessary software to launch an attached file, or if the reader only needs the text or data and doesn't need to format or alter the data in its original program.

Import versus Attach When you attach a file, that file remains in its original format (say, WordPad, 1-2-3, or Word for Windows, for example) and the file moves with the mail message to which you attach it. When you import a file (from WordPad or 1-2-3, for example), you convert the text so it works in Notes. The text becomes part of your mail message.

Table 9.1 lists the most common types of files you can import to Lotus Notes. For a more complete list, look in the Files of Type drop-down list in the Import dialog box.

TABLE 9.1 FILE TYPES NOTES CAN IMPORT

FILE TYPE	DESCRIPTION
Lotus 1-2-3, Symphony	Spreadsheet files
Ami Pro Document	Word processing files
ASCII Text	Text files
BMP, GIF, JPEG, PCX, and TIFF Images	Picture files
Excel 4, 5	Spreadsheet files (change to 1-2-3 before importing)
Word for Windows 6, 7	Word processing files

Follow these steps to import a file into your mail message:

1. In your mailbox, start or open the memo into which you want to import the text.
2. Position the insertion point within the brackets in the location where you want to insert the imported text.
3. Choose File, Import. The Import dialog box appears (see Figure 9.5).

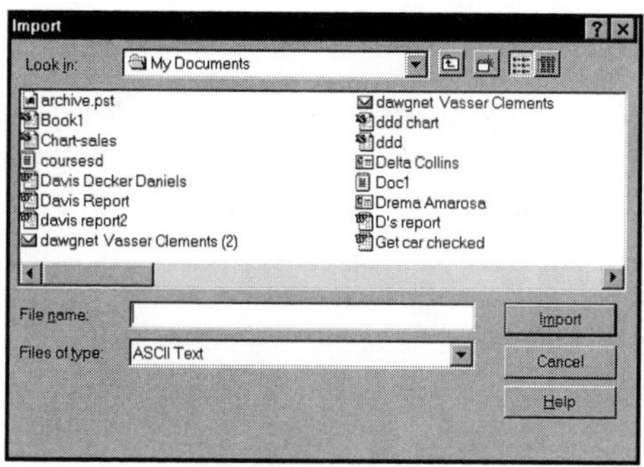

FIGURE 9.5 Select the file you want to import to the mail message.

4. In the Look in drop-down list, choose the folder in which the file resides.
5. In the list of files, select the file you want to import.
6. In the Files of type drop-down list, select the type of file you're importing.
7. Click the Import button, and Notes imports the file to the message.

Won't Accept File Type? If Notes displays a message saying the file type is not supported, you may need to go back into the original application and save the file in a different format, such as ASCII text. See the application's documentation for more information.

Notes imports the text into the message. You can now select the text, edit the text, or otherwise manipulate the text before you send the memo.

EXPORTING FILES

You can *export* any of your mail message files for use in another application. If you open the message before you export it, Notes offers more export options, such as WordPerfect and Ami Pro.

Export To convert a file to another file format, such as a format you can use in a word processing or spreadsheet application.

Table 9.2 lists the file types to which you can convert a Notes file for use in another application.

TABLE 9.2 FILE TYPES TO WHICH NOTES CAN CONVERT

FILE TYPE	DESCRIPTION
ASCII Text	Straight text
Ami Pro	Word processing file
CGM and TIFF	Picture files
Word for Windows 6, 7	Word processing files
WordPerfect 6.0, 6.1	Word processing files

It Doesn't Work You can use these file types only when reading or editing a memo.

To export a file from Notes, follow these steps:

1. In your mailbox, select the file you want to export and choose File, Export. The Export dialog box appears (see Figure 9.6).

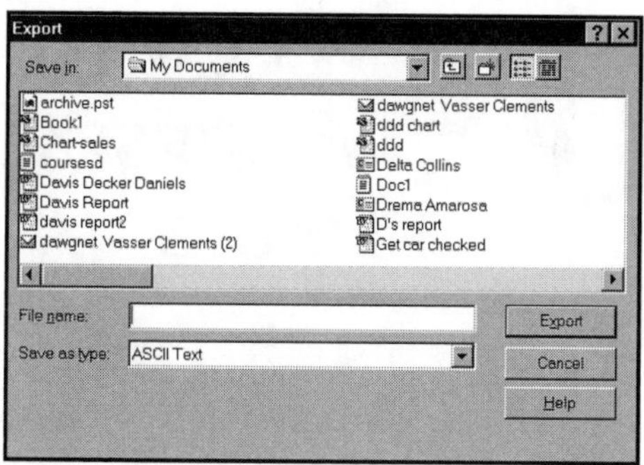

FIGURE 9.6 Choose a location and file name for the exported text file.

2. In the Save in drop-down list, choose a folder in which to save the exported file.
3. In the File name text box, enter a name for the exported file.
4. In the Save as type drop-down list, choose a file type to save the exported file as.
5. Choose Export. The file type Export dialog box appears.
6. When prompted, enter options depending on the selected file type.
7. When you finish setting the options, click OK in the Export dialog box. Notes exports a copy of the file to the location you selected. You can open the exported file(s) in an application that uses the designated file types.

In this lesson, you learned to organize your mail, attach files to mail messages, and import and export files to Notes. In the next lesson, you'll learn to manage workspace pages.

LESSON 10

Managing Workspace Pages

In this lesson, you learn to label page tabs, arrange workspace pages, locate database files, and add a database to a page.

Labeling Page Tabs

Notes provides six workspace pages you can use to store and organize your work in Notes, plus one page titled *Replicator*. You can label, or name, the workspace pages to suit you and your way of working.

Replicator The Replicator page contains tools you use to work remotely with Notes (when you're using a modem to attach to the network, for example). For more information on remote access to Notes, see Lesson 26.

The following steps walk you through labeling page tabs.

1. Select the page tab you want to label and double-click on the tab. The Properties for Workspace InfoBox appears (see Figure 10.1).
2. In the Tabs page of the Properties InfoBox, position the insertion point in the Workspace page name text box and enter a name.

What's in a Name? A workspace page name can contain as many as 32 characters, including letters, numbers, spaces, and other keyboard characters.

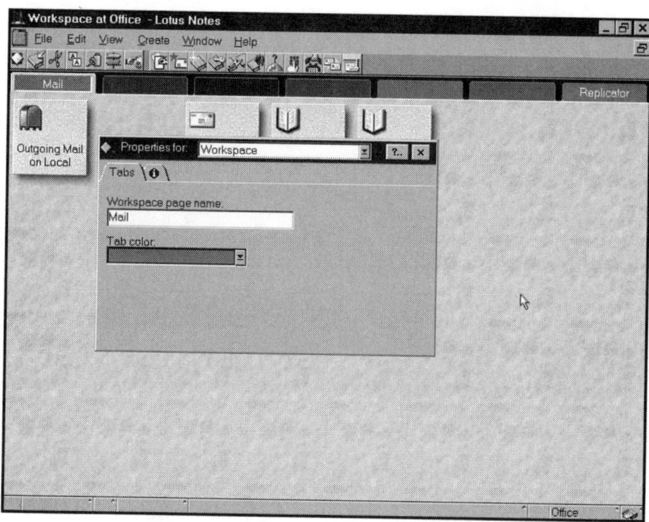

FIGURE 10.1 Use the Properties for Workspace InfoBox to name or rename a workspace page tab.

3. Press Enter to assign the page name. To close the InfoBox, click the Close (X) button.

Color You can click the Tab color drop-down arrow in the Properties for Workspace InfoBox and select a different color for the page tab, if you want.

ARRANGING ICONS ON THE WORKSPACE PAGE

Thus far in working with Notes, you've used your mailbox, your company's address book, and perhaps your personal address book to create and send mail throughout your network. On the workspace page, icons represent each of these items. You can move the icons around on your workspace pages to better organize your workspace, and you can move icons from page to page.

In addition, you can use the same methods to move other *databases* you access, copy, and create on your workspace.

Databases Databases contain documents; your address book is a database, for example. For more information about databases, see Lesson 11.

To move an icon on the same page, click and drag the icon to a new location. The mouse cursor changes to a hand while the mouse button is pressed in, and it changes back to a pointer when you release the button.

Overlap Icons If you drag one icon over the top of another, the two icons switch places.

To move an icon to another workspace page, click and drag the icon until the mouse pointer (a hand) is over the top of the page tab to which you want to move the icon. When you release the mouse button, the icon appears in the selected workspace page.

ADDING A DATABASE TO A PAGE

You can add a database to any of your workspace pages from either the server or your local drive. When you add a database, you're simply adding reference documents you can use in Notes. One database you might add, for example, may contain Help files. Another database might contain company files you need for a specific job.

To add a database to a page, follow these steps:

1. In your workspace, choose the page tab to which you want to add the database. Label the tab if you want.
2. Choose File, Database, Open. The Open Database dialog box appears (see Figure 10.2).

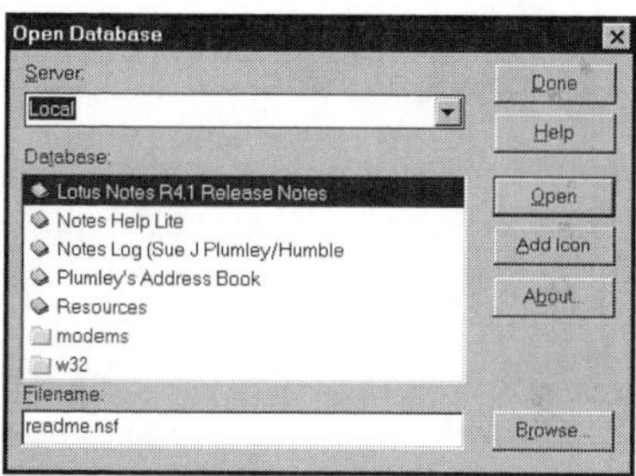

FIGURE 10.2 Add materials and documents to your workspace for easy access.

3. In the Server drop-down list, choose one of the following:

   Local Select this option to add a database from your own local drive.

   Other Select this option to view a list of available servers or computers from which you can choose. The Choose Other Server dialog box appears with a list of servers. Select one and click OK.

4. In the Database list, select the database you want to add to your workspace page.
5. If you cannot find the database you want in the Database list, click the Browse button. The Choose a Notes Database or Template File dialog box appears. Look through the available resources until you find the drive and folder that contain the database file you want to add. When you find the database, select it and click the Select button to return to the Open Database dialog box.
6. Click on one of the following command buttons:

   Done Closes the Open Database dialog box without adding a database to your workspace.

   Help Displays Help information on adding a database to your workspace.

Open Adds the database to your workspace and opens the database for you.

Add Icon Adds the database icon to your workspace and returns to the Open Database dialog box so you can select another database.

About Displays a preview window with the database showing so you can see if it's what you want. Click Close when you finish viewing the database to return to the Open Database dialog box.

7. If you're finished with the Open Database dialog box and it's still open, click Done. The database icon appears on your workspace page.

Can't Find a Database? Select one of the command buttons described in step 6 to complete the process.

Removing a Database from a Page

You can remove any database icon from the page. Removing the icon does not delete the database, so you can add the deleted database to your workspace page again at any time.

To delete a database icon from a page, right-click the icon to display the shortcut menu. Choose Remove from workspace, and the Lotus Notes confirmation dialog box appears. Click Yes to remove the icon, or click No to cancel the command.

In this lesson, you learned how to name workspace page tabs, arrange icons, add a database icon, and remove a database icon. In the next lesson, you'll learn to open and close a database as well as to understand a database.

USING DATABASES

LESSON 11

In this lesson, you'll gain an understanding of what a database is and how to use the database view, and you'll learn to open and close a database.

UNDERSTANDING DATABASES

In addition to using Notes for mailing messages to your co-workers, you can use Notes to share and access documents of various types. You might want to access your company's handbook, a colleague's sales reports, information on a new client or service, advertising letters, or any other important data you may need in order to complete your work.

A Notes database is not the same as what you would typically consider a database. You're probably used to the type of database you create with Access, Approach, or Q&A, in which you use fields to define such information as names, addresses, products, numbers, and prices. In Notes, however, related *documents* are stored in *databases*. The documents in a database can contain text, graphics, pictures, and other types of data. One Notes database you're already familiar with is your mailbox—a collection of documents you've received and sent.

Think of a database as a file folder; related documents are stored within the file folder. The creator of the database designates the types and designs of documents that are stored in the database. For example, advertising letters may be stored in one database, and quarterly sales figures may be stored in another.

Think of a workspace page as a file cabinet drawer containing several related databases or file folders. Use your six workspace pages to organize and manage different types of databases. You might use one page, for instance, for customer records and another page for product information.

You can access databases from your local drive and store them in your workspace pages. Two Notes databases already on your drive are the Help Lite files and your personal address book. You also can create and store your own databases on your local drive. You'll learn how to create your own databases and documents in Lesson 16.

Another feature enables you to access databases from any server available to you on your network. Your Domino server contains many default databases, including Help files and your company's address book. In addition, your supervisor, your Domino administrator, and perhaps some of your colleagues can add databases that you can access. If you're attached to other domains or Notes servers, you also may be able to access databases stored on those networks.

These are a few of the types of databases you may encounter:

- **Information Services** Current or updated data about your company, new products, procedures, services, employees, and policies.
- **Document Libraries** Forms, reports, memos, and other document types you would normally find on paper are stored electronically in a document library database.
- **Discussion Databases** Online written discussions between you and your colleagues in which you share ideas, solve problems, and discuss current events (or whatever else you want). For more information, see Lesson 14.

If you're used to working in a word processing or spreadsheet program, you're used to saving one document as a file. In Notes, however, the entire database—including all of its documents—is saved as a file. A database full of documents is like a word processing file full of paragraphs. So when you want to copy or delete a document from a database, for example, you have to copy or delete all documents in the database because they are all part of the saved file.

OPENING A DATABASE

All databases display similar elements and views. Depending on the type of database you open, you'll see general views (such as All Documents, Folders and Views, and so on) and specific views that apply only to the database. For example, a document library database may contain such views as My Favorite Documents, Archive Logs, and Review Stats.

To open a database already on your workspace page, double-click the database's icon. Alternatively, you can right-click the database icon and choose Open.

New Database For information about adding a new database to your workspace, see Lesson 10.

VIEWING THE ABOUT DOCUMENT

The first time you open many databases, an About document appears. The About document displays information about the database you're about to view, and it appears only the first time you access a database. The About document is created by the person who created the database. For example, suppose your department head creates a database full of departmental forms such as expense reports, referral forms, and timesheets. She might then create an About document that describes each form and explains when you can use it.

When you create your own database in Lesson 16, you'll also create an About document. Figure 11.1 shows the About document for a database about new training services that was created for the Humble Opinions company.

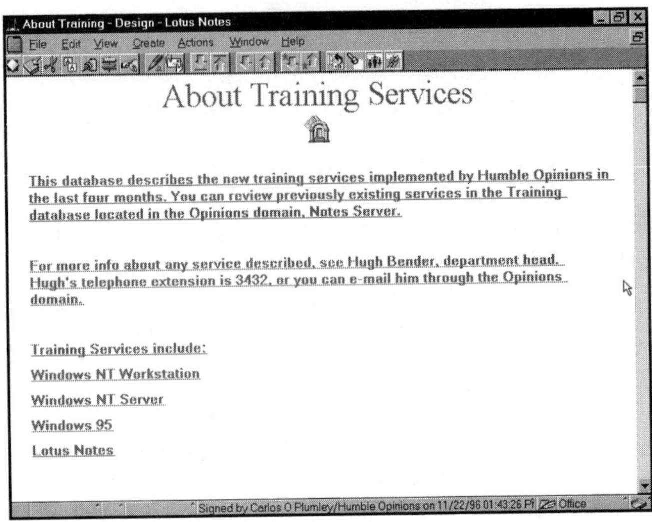

FIGURE 11.1 Read the About document for more information about the database you opened.

When you've finished viewing the About document, choose File, Close to close it and open the database.

Oops You can access the About document again at any time. Simply open the database and choose Help, About This Database. The About document appears. Choose File, Close to close the document again when you're done.

VIEWING THE DATABASE

When you close the About document, the database appears (see Figure 11.2). You'll recognize many elements of the database window because it is similar to your mailbox window. All databases contain similar elements.

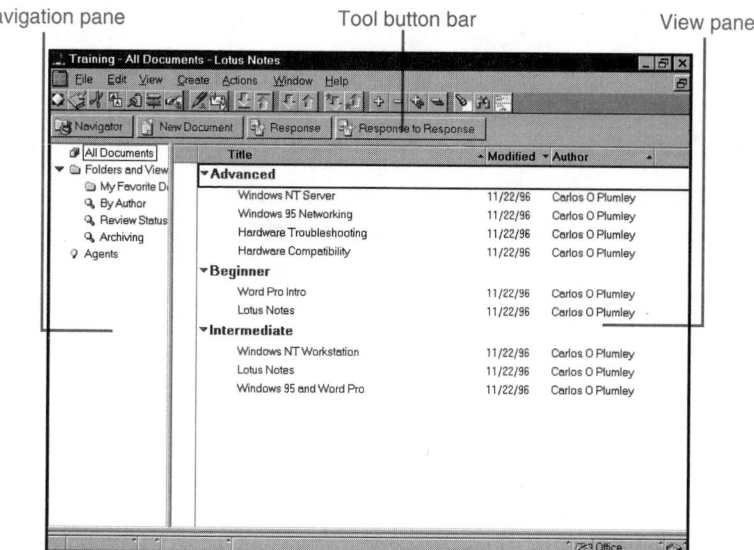

FIGURE 11.2 Each database contains some unique views and elements.

When working in a database, just as in your mailbox database, you select a view in the navigation pane by clicking once on that view. A right arrow beside a view means you can display more related topics by clicking that arrow. When all views are displayed, the arrow changes to a down arrow, which you can click to hide the related views. Click once on any view to select it. A rectangular outline appears around a selected view, and the items in the view pane change.

In the view pane, a right arrow beside a *category* represents hidden document titles. You must click the arrow beside the category to display the document titles. Click the arrow a second time to hide the related topics. For more information about viewing a database, see Lesson 12.

Category In a database, a category describes the documents filed within that particular database. You cannot open the category like a document, but you can expand or collapse it by clicking the arrow beside it. When it is expanded, the titles of the documents within the category appear.

CLOSING A DATABASE

When you're finished with a database, close it by choosing File, Close or by pressing Ctrl+W. If you've added documents or made any changes to the existing database, Notes will prompt you to save. Click Yes to save your changes; click No to abandon the changes; click Cancel to return to the database.

Don't Close If you don't want to close the database but you need to do something else in Notes, such as work in your mailbox or view your workspace, you can leave the database open. To switch to the workspace, choose Window, Workspace at Office. To switch to another open database, choose Window and the name of that database.

In this lesson, you learned to open and close a database and to work in the database window. In the next lesson, you'll learn about database templates, and you'll learn how to view and manipulate documents in the document window.

WORKING WITH A DATABASE

In this lesson, you learn about database templates and how to view documents in the view pane, mark documents, and print documents.

UNDERSTANDING TEMPLATES

Each database in Domino is based on a *template* of some sort. The template governs how the database looks when you open it. Although all databases have a navigation pane and a view pane, the template supplies tool button bars and various views in the database. Therefore, when you use a template, you can have several different databases that all display the same elements.

Template A formatted design for a database that governs how the documents and the database view look. Each template displays different views, tool button bars, and options. In addition to the templates supplied by Domino, your Domino administrator may create his or her own templates to use with company documents.

Figure 12.1 displays a document library database for a company called Humble Opinions. The tool buttons represent actions you can take while in this particular database. Likewise, the views in the navigation pane (on the left side of the screen) show various collections of the documents in the database.

Figure 12.2 shows a database based on the room reservations template, which is used for reserving company meeting rooms at specific times. The tool buttons and navigation pane are different from those in the template shown in Figure 12.1.

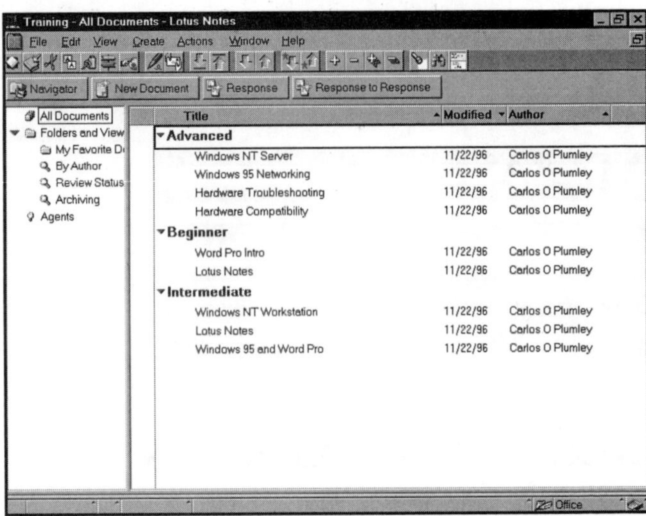

FIGURE 12.1 A document library displays the documents, views, and tools available in this database.

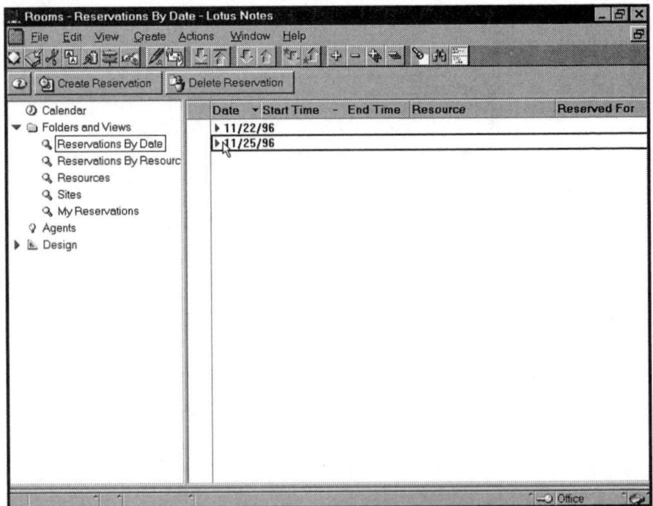

FIGURE 12.2 Each database offers different views and tool buttons.

Help If you open a database and you're not sure how to view or use it, choose Help, Using This Database for instructions about using the database. Choose File, Close to close the Help window when you're done.

VIEWING DOCUMENTS IN THE VIEW PANE

Most Domino databases offer similar tools for accessing help when viewing the documents in the database. In the view pane (on the right), a set of buttons describe what you see on-screen—for example, the Title, Modification Date, Resource, and Time. Depending on the database type, you can rearrange, or sort, the documents in the view pane using these buttons.

To arrange documents in the view pane of a database, follow these steps:

1. Click the Title button in the view pane. The document titles appear in alphabetical order, as shown in Figure 12.3. (The database in the figure is based on a Journal template—one in which you can record personal or professional information.)
2. Click the Modified button in the view pane to arrange the entries by the modification or creation dates, from most recent to least recent.
3. (Optional) If your database lists the name of the last person to modify each document, click the Modified By button to alphabetize the files by those names.

Don't Miss Any Some databases display documents by categories, dates, or locations only. You can choose the View, Expand All menu command to make sure you see all documents in the database.

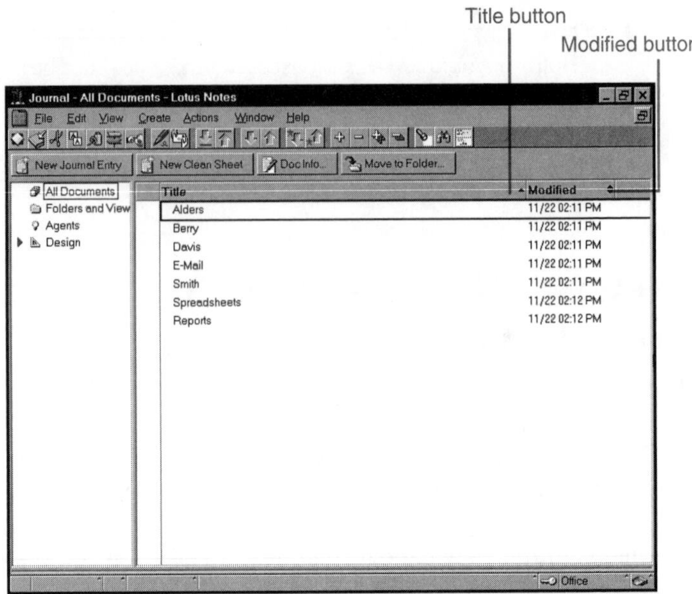

FIGURE 12.3 List documents in alphabetical order so you can easily find the one you want.

MANIPULATING DOCUMENTS

You can print, cut, edit, or otherwise manipulate many documents in a database, depending on the type of database and whether you have access control to edit or cut documents from it. (See Lesson 13 for more information about access control.) Before you can perform some actions (such as printing), you must select, or *mark*, the document(s) you want to work with. You select documents in the view pane before you open any document.

Mark a Document Marking is a method of designating a document for the next action, such as deleting, editing, or copying. Marking is the same as selecting.

Open a Document Open a document by double-clicking the document's title in the database. You'll learn more about opening a document in Lesson 15.

MARKING DOCUMENTS

You mark the document or documents on which you want to perform an action. To mark a document, click in the column to the left of the document title. A check mark appears beside the marked document, as shown in Figure 12.4. To remove the mark from a document, simply click on the check mark.

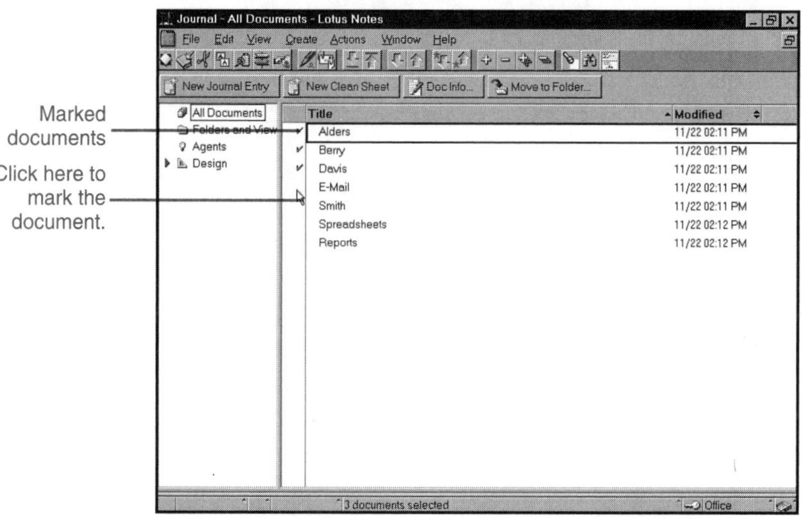

FIGURE 12.4 Mark documents on which you want to perform an action.

PRINTING MARKED DOCUMENTS

You can print the documents you've marked without opening them. To print marked documents, follow these steps:

1. Mark the documents you want to print. Then right-click on one of the marked documents, and the shortcut menu appears.
2. Choose Print. The File Print dialog box appears (see Figure 12.5).

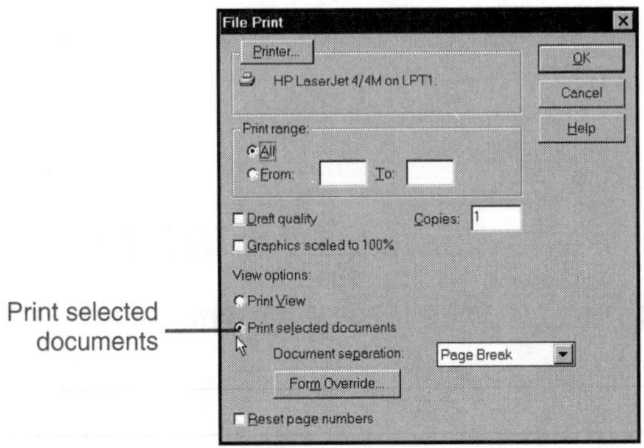

FIGURE 12.5 Tell Notes to print only the marked documents.

3. Choose Print selected documents and choose a Document separation mark from that drop-down list. Choosing this option is the same as placing a page break between the documents. (For more information about printing a document, see Lesson 6.)
4. Click OK to print the selected documents.

Copy a Document? The only way to copy a specific document from a database is to right-click the document and choose Copy from the shortcut menu. You can then paste the document into another database. You also can copy an entire database of documents (see Lesson 13).

In this lesson, you learned about database templates and how to view and manipulate documents in the view pane. In the next lesson, you'll learn to copy, scan, and remove a database.

LESSON 13

MANAGING DATABASES

In this lesson, you learn about access rights. You also learn to scan a database for unread documents, read those documents, and remove a database.

UNDERSTANDING ACCESS RIGHTS

Domino enables you to perform certain tasks in a database—such as editing, deleting, and copying—only if you have rights to do so. Either the creator of a database or the database manager decides and assigns access rights to the users of the database. Some people may be allowed to create documents for the database, and others may be allowed only to read documents from the database.

The manager of a database assigns rights to various people through the *access control list*. The manager can assign any of seven user access levels, each of which brings with it certain privileges. The following list describes each user access level in an access control list:

- **Manager** The manager has the right to perform any and all functions within the database, including assigning access rights to others on the network and deleting the database.
- **Designer** The designer can create, modify, and delete documents, as well as create and modify forms and views.
- **Editor** The editor can create, modify, and delete documents in a database, including documents created by others.

- **Author** The author can create and read documents. An author can modify his or her own documents, but he or she can only read others' documents.
- **Reader** A reader can only read documents in the database.
- **Depositor** A depositor can only add items to a database.
- **No Access** Prevents the user from performing operations within a document or accessing the document at all.

Forms and Views Designing and creating forms and views is part of designing your own database, which is beyond the scope of this book. To learn more about designing your own database, pick up Que's *Special Edition Using Lotus Notes*. On the other hand, creating a database and documents is covered in Lesson 16.

Your access rights may vary from one database to another. To find out your access rights in any database, click the Access button on the Status bar (the third button from the right). The Status bar's message area displays your access level, as shown in Figure 13.1. In addition, the Groups and Roles dialog box appears, in which you can view your access level. Click Done to close the dialog box.

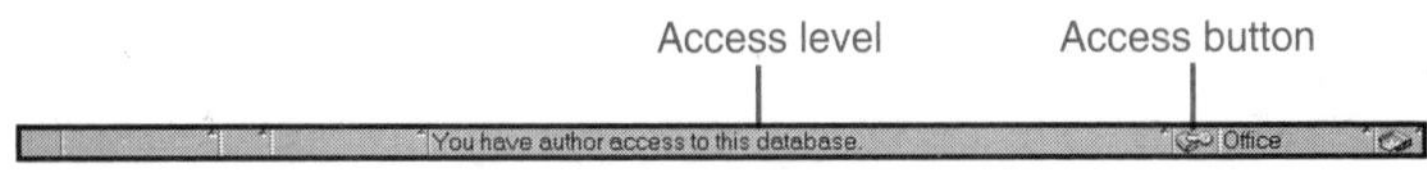

FIGURE 13.1 The Status bar shows your level of access rights.

As you work with databases and documents, remember that you may not have the access you need to perform all procedures you want to perform.

COPYING A DATABASE

You can copy a database from your local drive to another folder cr drive, or from a server to your local drive. You might want to copy a database for easier access or availability, for example. To copy a database to another location, follow these steps:

1. In the open database, choose File, Database, New Copy. The Copy Database dialog box appears (see Figure 13.2).

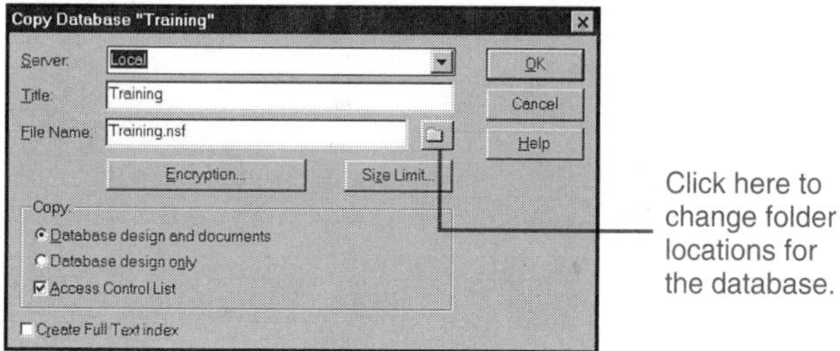

FIGURE 13.2 You can copy a database and all of its documents, but not just one or two documents from a database.

2. In the Server drop-down list, choose either Local or the server to which you want to copy the database.
3. In the Title text box, use the original title or enter another name for the database.
4. In the File Name text box, use the default file name or enter a new one. If necessary, click the folder icon to change locations. Notes displays the Choose a folder dialog box shown in Figure 13.3.
5. Choose a drive and folder in which to place the copied database and click OK.
6. Click OK again in the Copy Database dialog box, and Notes copies the database. Notes also adds a database icon for the copied database to the active workspace page.

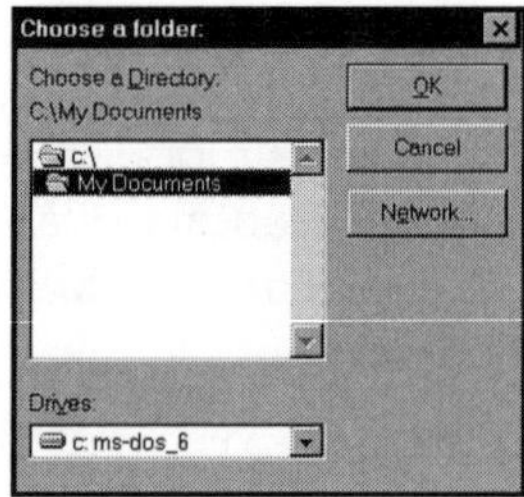

Figure 13.3 Copy the file to your local drive for your own personal use.

Move the Icon If you want, you can move the copied database icon from one workspace page to another by clicking and dragging the icon to any page tab in your workspace.

Scanning a Database

If your company uses many databases in which documents are added and updated daily, you may want to use the Notes scan feature to locate documents you have not yet read. This saves you from having to wade through each database every day.

Identifying the Databases

Before you can scan databases, you must identify those databases to Notes. Make sure no databases are selected, and then follow these steps:

1. In your workspace, choose Edit, Unread Marks, Scan Unread. The Scan Unread dialog box appears (see Figure 13.4).
2. Click the Choose Preferred button. The Scan Unread Preferred Setup dialog box appears (see Figure 13.5).

FIGURE 13.4 Choose which databases you want to scan for new or updated documents.

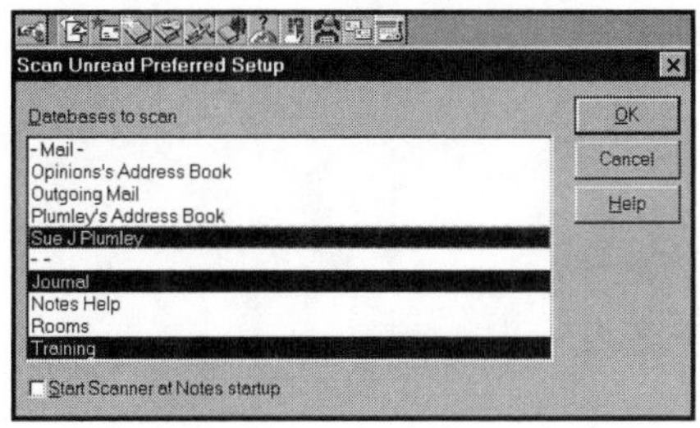

FIGURE 13.5 Scan those databases you use the most.

3. Select the databases you want to scan. Notes automatically scans any database with a hyphen in front of it.
4. (Optional) Choose the Start Scanner at Notes startup check box if you want Notes to scan automatically each time you start the program.
5. Click OK to return to the Scan Unread dialog box. Choose Done.

SCANNING AND READING

You can scan one database or multiple databases for new additions. Follow these steps to scan the database.

1. In the workspace page, choose View, Show Unread. A box appears in each database icon showing the number of unread documents in that database (see Figure 13.6).
2. To refresh the scanned view at any time, choose View, Refresh Unread Count.

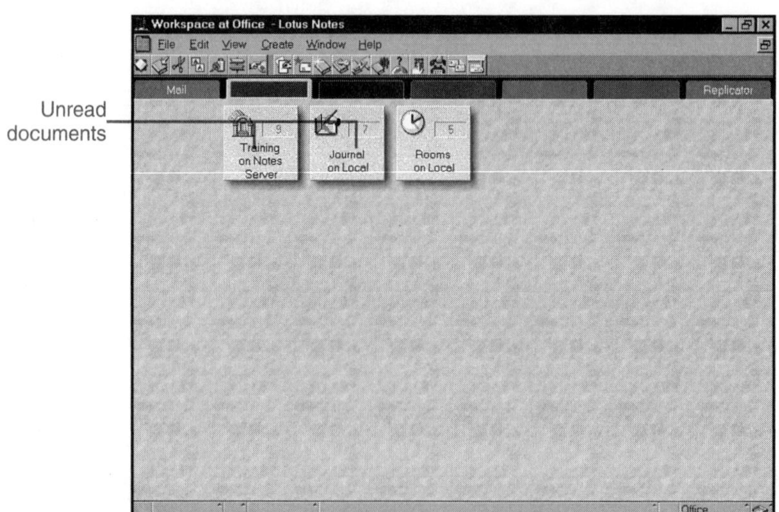

FIGURE 13.6 Each icon shows the number of unread documents.

3. To read unread documents in a database, select the database and choose Edit, Unread Marks, Scan Unread. The first document appears for you to read.

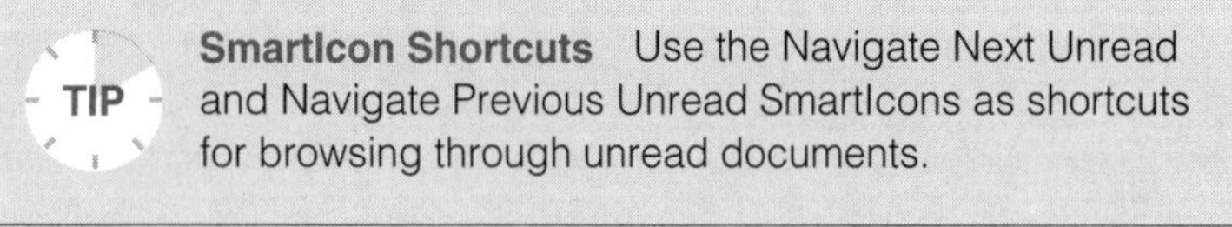

SmartIcon Shortcuts Use the Navigate Next Unread and Navigate Previous Unread SmartIcons as shortcuts for browsing through unread documents.

4. Close that document, and the next unread document appears.

5. Repeat step 4 until Notes has displayed all unread documents in the database.

REMOVING A DATABASE

You can remove any database from a workspace page. To do so, right-click on the database to reveal the shortcut menu, choose

Remove from Workspace, and choose Yes in the confirmation dialog box. Notes removes the database icon, but the database data remains on the local or network drive.

To remove a database from your local drive, open the Windows Explorer, select the database file you want to remove (look for NSF extensions), and press the Delete key. Confirm the deletion, and then close the Windows Explorer.

When using NT 4 with Domino databases, you must have permission to use the server. If you have trouble accessing any database on the server, see your Domino or system administrator.

In this lesson, you learned about access control. In addition, you learned how to copy a database, scan a database for unread documents, read those documents, and remove a database from a workspace page. In the next lesson, you'll learn how to join a discussion group.

Lesson 14 Joining a Discussion Group

In this lesson, you'll learn to join a discussion group, post a message, answer a message, and exit the group.

Joining the Group

A *discussion group* is a database shared among those in your workgroup and is usually focused on one topic, such as an advertising campaign, a new product line, or some other special interest. Think of a discussion group as an informal meeting place where you can share your ideas on the subject at hand.

When you join a discussion group, you add your comments, questions, theories, and so on to those of your coworkers. All discussion is stored in a database that you can open and read like any other. To join a discussion group, follow these steps:

1. In your Notes workspace, choose File, Database, Open. The Open Database dialog box appears (see Figure 14.1).

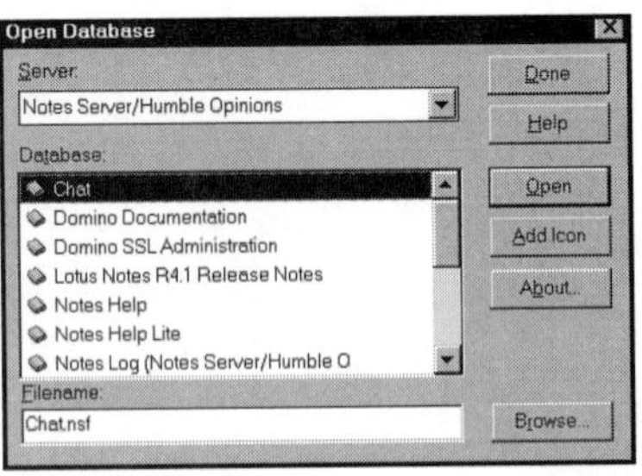

Figure 14.1 The Open Database dialog box gives you access to discussion groups.

2. In the Server drop-down list, choose the server on which the discussion group database resides. If you're not sure where the database is located, use the Browse button to access the network. (You can also ask your Domino administrator if you cannot find the database.)
3. In the Database list, select the discussion group database. Ask your Notes administrator for the name of the database if you're unsure.
4. Click the Add Icon button.
5. Choose Done. Notes adds the database to your workspace.
6. To open the discussion group database, double-click its icon on your workspace. Notes opens the database. Figure 14.2 shows an example discussion group database.

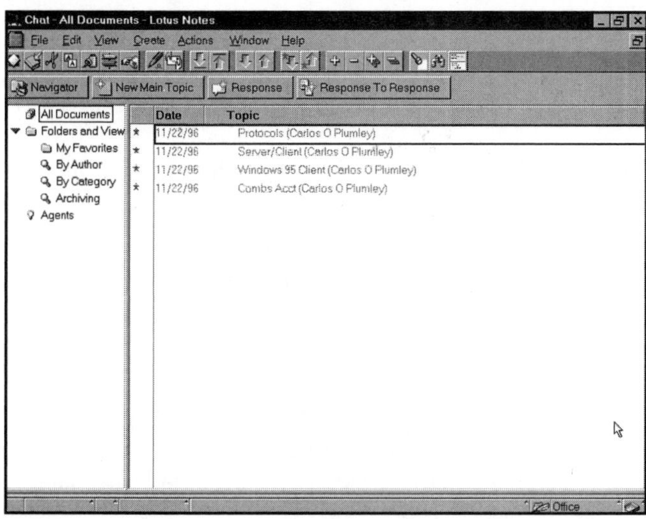

FIGURE 14.2 A discussion database lists main topics for discussion.

VIEWING THE DISCUSSION WINDOW

The navigation pane (on the left side of the discussion database window) provides several views you can use to find and organize messages. The default view is the All Documents view shown in Figure 14.2. The All Documents view displays all messages in the database listed by date, topic, and author. You can rearrange the topics by clicking the Date button in the document pane. By default, Notes sorts the messages from the most recent to the oldest dates. If the items in your navigation pane look different from those in the figure, click the Navigator button on the tool button bar.

The second view, My Favorite Documents, looks just like the All Documents view. The difference between My Favorite Documents and All Documents is that My Favorite Documents view displays fewer messages because you save only the messages you want. If you run across an important or particularly interesting message in the All Documents view, you can click and drag it to the My Favorite Documents icon in the view pane. Notes copies the message for you to keep.

In the third view, By Author, Notes displays a list of all documents by one author directly under that person's name. The date and the topic of the message are also displayed.

The fourth view is By Category. All messages stored in the database are created within a specific category, or section. To view the categories, click the By Category icon.

Icons in the Navigation Pane Some databases enable you to display the views by icon instead of by standard folders. To change the look of the view pane, click the Navigator tool button. To change back to the default view, click the Standard Folders button.

POSTING A MESSAGE

You can join a discussion group by opening the database and reading messages from those in the group, or you can compose your own messages to add to the discussion. To post a new message to a discussion group, follow these steps:

1. In the discussion database, click the New Main Topic tool button. The New Topic window appears (see Figure 14.3).

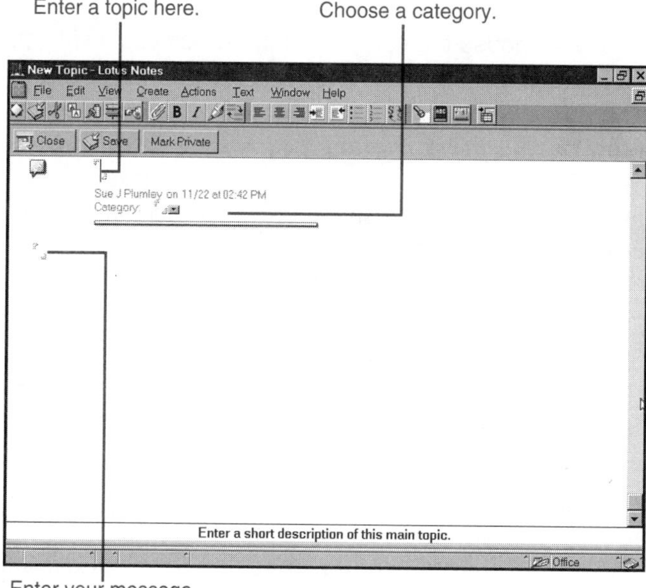

FIGURE 14.3 Create your own messages to add to the discussion.

2. Enter a topic in the first set of brackets. The topic is the name of your message, and it is what Notes displays in the database window.
3. Click the down arrow next to Category to choose the category in which your message fits. The Select Keywords dialog box appears, with General selected by default (see Figure 14.4). A document may fit into one, two, three, or more categories at the same time.

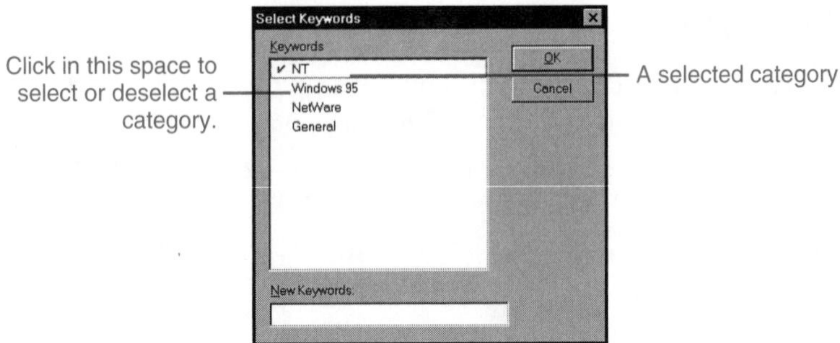

FIGURE 14.4 Choose the category under which you want your message listed.

4. In the Keywords list, click on the keyword for the category to which you want to assign your message. Notes displays a check mark beside it. You can click on a selected category to deselect it and remove the check mark. When you're satisfied with your choice, click OK.

Add a Keyword If you want to add a keyword to make it a category, enter it in the New Keywords text box in the Select Keywords dialog box. Press Enter to add the category and close the dialog box.

5. Position the insertion point between the text brackets and enter your message.
6. When you finish entering the message, click the Save tool button.
7. Click the Close tool button to return to the discussion group database.

READING AND REPLYING TO A MESSAGE

In addition to creating messages, you'll want to read the messages from others and reply to them. You can respond to a message from the message itself or from the database window. Follow these steps to read and respond to a message.

1. From the database window, double-click any message you want to read. Notes opens the message, displaying the topic, author, date, and category at the top (see Figure 14.5).

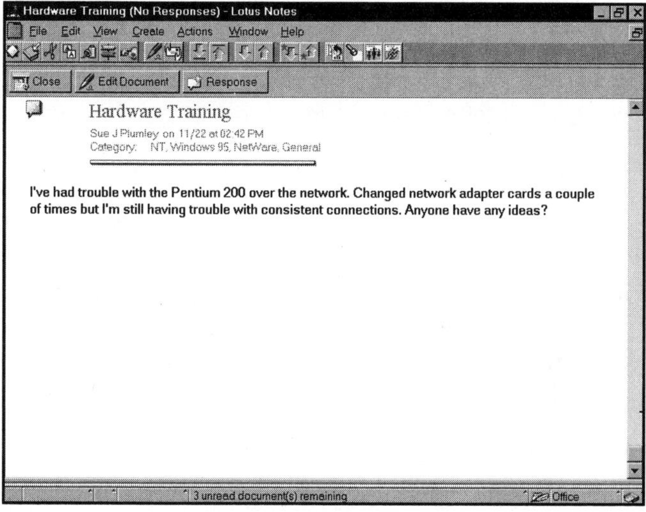

FIGURE 14.5 Open a message and read it, and then respond to it or close it.

2. To respond to the message, choose the Response tool button. The New Response window shown in Figure 14.6 appears.

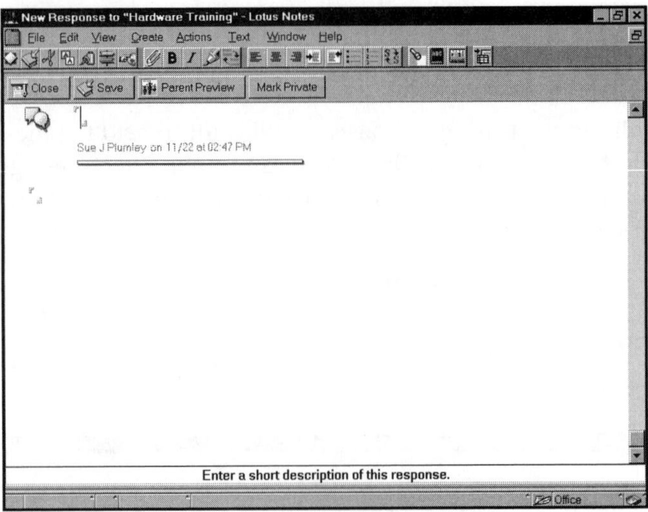

FIGURE 14.6 Enter a message in response to the one you just read.

3. Enter your topic and your message in the New Response window.
4. (Optional) If you need to refer to the original message, click the Parent Preview button on the tool button bar. The screen splits in half so you can see both the original message and your response.
5. When you finish the response, click Save and then Close.
6. Close the original message to return to the discussion database window.

You've Got a Reply! In the discussion database window, responses appear directly below the original message and in a different color. In addition, Notes displays the number of responses you've received to your messages beside your name.

Response to a Response? In the database window, you can respond to a message without opening it. Simply select the message and choose the Response tool button to display the New Response window. Click the Response to Response button to reply to a message that's a response to an original.

EXITING THE GROUP

You close the discussion group database as you would any other database. Choose File, Close to return to the workspace. If you have created messages but have not saved them, Notes displays a confirmation dialog box prompting you to save. Choose Yes to save the messages you've created.

In this lesson, you learned to join a discussion group, post a message, answer a message, and exit the group. In the next lesson, you'll learn to work with documents within databases by opening them, marking them, and moving around in the documents.

Lesson 15 Working with Documents

In this lesson, you learn to open a document, move from document to document, mark a document as read, and exit a document.

Opening a Document

Select the document you want to open from the document window of any database. To open a document, double-click on it, or right-click it and choose Open from the shortcut menu. Figure 15.1 shows an open document from a library database named "Training."

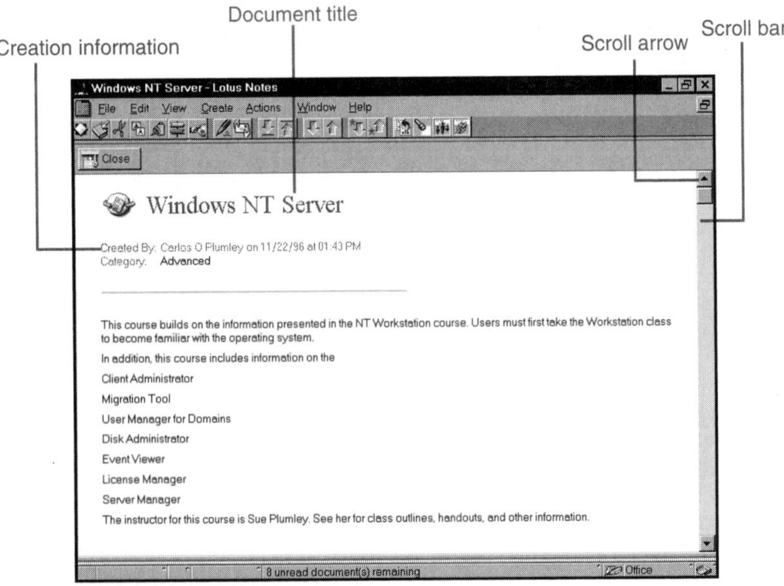

Figure 15.1 Open a document to read the data in it.

In the open document, you can use the scroll bar to view any of the document that's not displayed in the window. Click the scroll arrows to move up or down in the document one line at a time.

Shortcuts You can also move around in a document by pressing the Page Up and Page Down keys.

Moving from Document to Document

You can move to the next or previous document in a database without closing the current document and returning to the database. To do so, you use the SmartIcons in the document window. The following list shows those SmartIcons and explains their functions.

Use the Navigate Next icon to move to the next document listed in the database.

The Navigate Previous icon moves you to the previous document in the database.

Use the Navigate Next Unread icon to move to the next unread document in the database.

The Navigate Previous Unread icon moves you to an unread document previous to the current one.

If the database does not contain a document that matches your request (if there is not a next unread document, for example), Notes returns to the database view. See the next section for more information about marking documents as read or unread.

Marking a Document as Read

Many databases will contain so many documents that it's difficult to keep track of the ones you've read. Notes provides a way for you to mark the documents you've read so you don't waste time opening them again. You can also use marking options to help you organize and manage the documents in a database.

In order to see marked documents, you must be in the database view window. A red star appears beside each unread document; no mark at all indicates that you've read (or at least opened) that document. Figure 15.2 shows six unread documents.

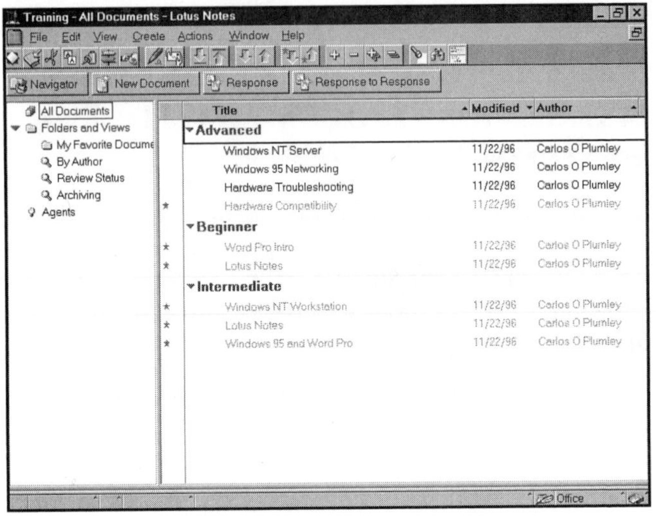

FIGURE 15.2 A red star marks each unread document.

To mark documents in the database view, choose Edit, Unread Marks, and then choose one of the following marking options:

Mark Selected Read Marks any documents you select as read; unread documents remain unmarked and easy to find.

Mark All Read Marks all documents in a database as read; this makes it easy to find new documents added to the database.

Mark Selected Unread Marks selected documents as unread, which is useful if you need to be reminded to re-read important documents in a database.

Mark All Unread Marks all documents in the database as unread.

Scan Unread You can choose Edit, Unread Marks, Scan Unread to quickly view only the unread documents in a database. See Lesson 13 to learn more about scanning.

EDITING A DOCUMENT

Sometimes you will need to edit the documents in a database. You can add or delete text or graphics in a document, and you can *format* the documents. The following steps walk you through the basics of editing a document. For information about formatting documents, see Lesson 18.

Format To change certain visual characteristics of a document. This might include changing fonts or type sizes, making text bold or italic, or aligning the text on the page.

Editing Others' Documents You cannot edit others' documents unless you have permission to do so. If you cannot edit a document, see your Notes administrator.

1. In the database, open the document you want to edit.
2. Right-click anywhere within the document and choose Edit from the shortcut menu, or simply double-click in the text area of the document. Brackets appear, marking areas in which you can make changes (see Figure 15.3).
3. Enter or edit the text within brackets.
4. When you finish editing, choose File, Save.

Bracket

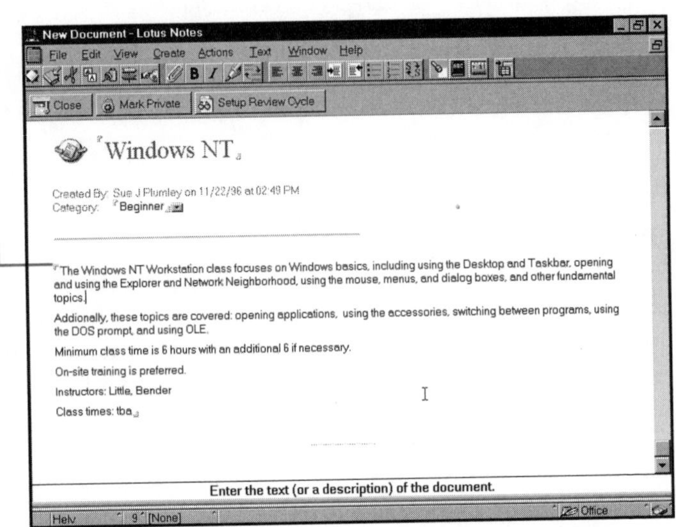

FIGURE 15.3 Edit a document by positioning the insertion point between the brackets.

EXITING A DOCUMENT

When you're finished reading a document, you should close it. Multiple open documents clutter your Notes work area and can slow down your computer's reaction time. To close, or exit, a document, choose File, Close or click the Close tool button.

Save Before Closing If you forgot to save changes you made to the document, Notes prompts you to save before it closes the document. Click Yes to save the changes, click No to close without saving the changes, or click Cancel to return to the document.

In this lesson, you learned to open and exit a document, to move among documents in a database, and to mark a document as read. In the next lesson, you will learn to create a document in a database.

LESSON 16

Creating a Database and Documents

In this lesson, you learn to create a database, create documents, and delete a document.

Creating a Database

You can create your own database in which to store documents for your personal use on your local drive, or for use on the network. As creator of the database, you can choose the document types that go into the database, and you can compose any or all of the documents in your database. To create a database, follow these steps:

1. In your workspace, choose File, Database, New. The New Database dialog box appears (see Figure 16.1).

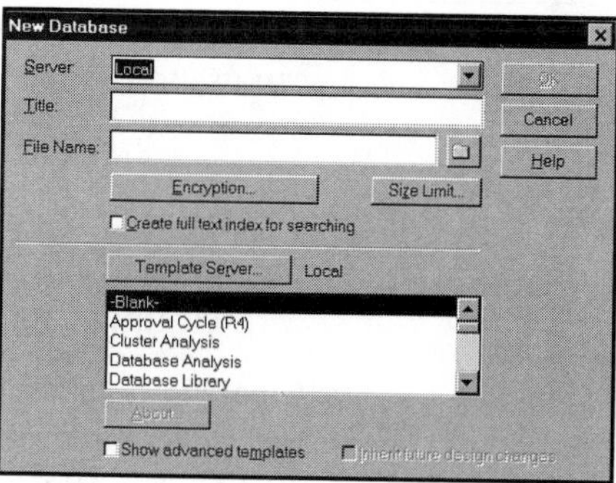

Figure 16.1 Create your own databases and documents.

2. In the Server drop-down list, choose the local drive or the network drive to which you want to save the database.

3. In the Title text box, enter a name for the database. Notes automatically fills in the File Name text box as you enter the title.
4. In the list at the bottom of the dialog box, choose a template on which to base your new database. (Table 16.1 describes some of the available templates.) Click the Template Server button to view templates the Notes administrator may have created for your use.
5. Click OK. Notes creates an icon on the current workspace and opens the new database for you.

Need More Template Choices? You can click the Show advanced templates check box in the New Database dialog box to access more templates from which you can choose.

TABLE 16.1 COMMON DATABASE TEMPLATES

TEMPLATE	DESCRIPTION
Blank	Creates an empty database you can use to create anything from documents to views to the design of the template. (I do not recommend that you choose this unless you're experienced with creating databases.)
Discussion	Creates a database you can use for discussion groups for specific groups of people—such as instructors, salespeople, or advertising agents. (See Lesson 14 for details on discussion groups.)

TEMPLATE	DESCRIPTION
Document Library	Creates a database in which you can store reference documents such as handouts, financial statements, or product descriptions. This is for access by a workgroup.
Personal Address Book	Creates a personal address book for your local drive.
Personal Journal	Creates a database that contains documents in which you can enter any data you want, including notes, To Do lists, and other topics of interest.
Resource Reservations	Creates a database in which workgroups can reserve and schedule the use of such company resources as meeting rooms, company cars, and office equipment.

Need Help? To learn more about any template, click the About button in the New Database dialog box to view the About document on the selected database. Choose Close when you finish with the About document.

CREATING AN ABOUT DOCUMENT

When you first create a database from a template, the About document appears. The About document describes the database template and its uses and provides other relative information about it. Figure 16.2 shows an example of an About document.

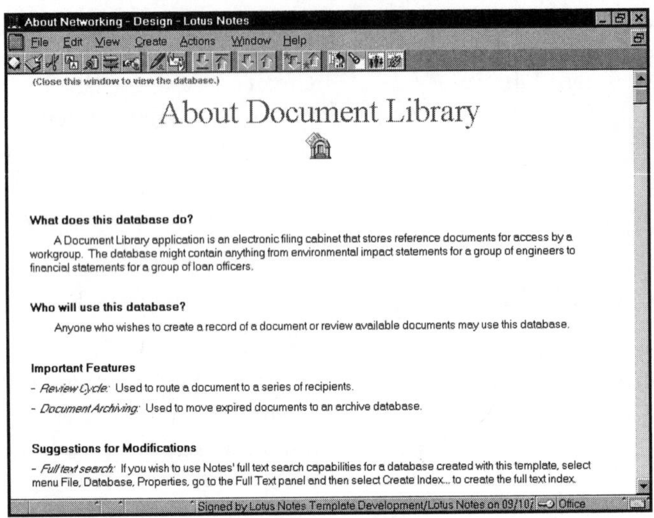

FIGURE 16.2 The About document describes the template's uses.

You can leave the information in an About document as it is, or you can edit the document and enter your own information. When creating an About document, you might want to enter such information as:

- Descriptions of the documents
- The names of groups or users who can edit or access the documents
- Guidelines to follow when using the documents
- The name and e-mail address or phone number of someone who can help users with the database

To create your own About document, follow these steps:

1. In the About document that appears when the database opens, right-click anywhere in the document and choose Edit.

2. Click anywhere in the document and enter, edit, or delete the text.
3. When you finish making changes, choose File, Save to save your changes to the About document.
4. Choose File, Close to view the new database.

COMPOSING A DOCUMENT

You might need to create a document for your own database or for a database you've accessed over the network. For example, you might create reports or articles in your own database that you want to share with your co-workers, or your company may require you to submit status reports or other information to a *public* database.

Public Database A database that is accessible to anyone on the network. Some databases may be marked as private or completely inaccessible, and others may have limits set by the network or Notes administrators that enable only certain groups to access them. In a similar way, you can create a private folder in a database and limit access to that folder and the documents it contains, and you can encrypt certain documents within a database. However, those topics are beyond the scope of this book. For more information, see Que's *Special Edition Using Lotus Notes.*

Whether you're adding a document to an existing database or creating your own database documents, the procedure is the same. Follow these steps to create a document.

1. In the database view, choose the location for the new document from the view pane. You might choose to place the document in the All Documents view or in a specific folder, for example.

2. Click the New Document button on the tool button bar. A new document like the one in Figure 16.3 appears.

Sound Familiar? The process of creating a new document may sound familiar to you because it's similar to creating a message in a discussion group database (which you learned about in Lesson 14). You also can import and export data in a database document just as you would with mail (see Lesson 9).

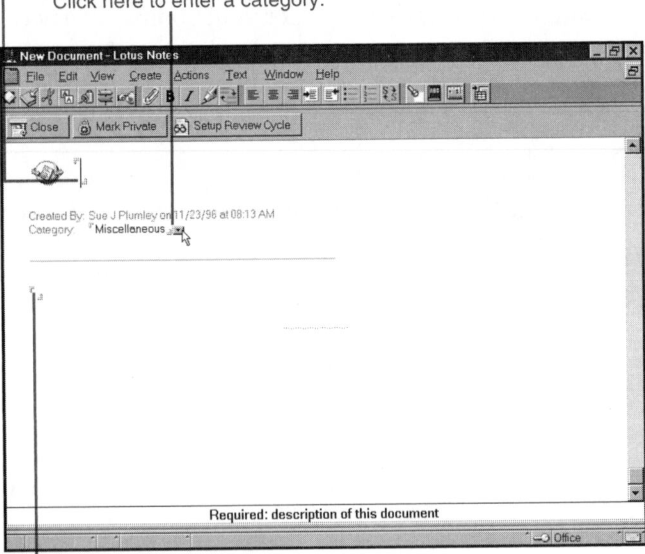

FIGURE 16.3 Enter your own document title and text.

3. In the first set of brackets, enter the title for the document. This title will appear in the document window of the database view.

4. For the category, you can leave Miscellaneous as the selection, or you can click the down arrow to reveal the Select Keywords dialog box (see Figure 16.4).

Categories Categories are main topics into which you organize your documents. Some example categories might be Quarter 1 and Quarter 2, or Expenses and Income. Categories appear in the database view with the associated documents listed below them.

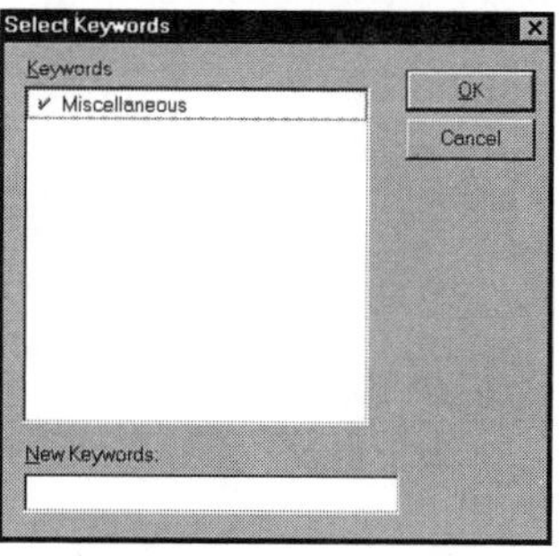

FIGURE 16.4 Select a keyword to use as the category, or enter a new keyword.

5. In the Keywords list, click on a category. A check mark appears beside it to show that it's selected. To deselect a marked keyword, click on it, and the check mark disappears.

   If there are no categories, or if you do not see a category you want to use, enter the name of a new category in the New Keywords text box.

6. Choose OK to apply the keyword.

7. Click inside the third set of brackets and enter the document text.

Formatting a Document For more information about formatting—applying fonts, text characteristics, and so on—see Lesson 18.

SAVING A DOCUMENT

When you're finished creating a document, you must save it to the database. To save a document, choose File, Save. You can then close the document by clicking the Close button in the tool button bar. When you close the document, Notes returns to the database view.

Oops! If you try to close the document without saving it, Notes prompts you to save your changes. Click Yes to save the document, click No to abandon the changes, or click Cancel to return to the document.

DELETING A DOCUMENT

If you no longer need a particular document, you can delete it from the database view. Simply right-click on the document and choose Cut from the shortcut menu that appears. The document disappears from the database, but it's not completely gone. Notes moves the document you cut to the Clipboard, which means you can paste it back into your database for as long as it remains on the Clipboard. A cut or copied document remains on the Clipboard until you cut or copy another item. To retrieve the cut document, choose Edit, Paste.

In this lesson, you learned to create a database, compose a document, save a document, and delete a document. In the next lesson, you will learn to work with text fields.

LESSON 17

Editing Text Fields

In this lesson, you learn about text fields. You also learn how to move around in a document, select text, and move and copy text in a document.

Understanding Text Fields

When you enter text into a mail memo, a discussion group message, or a document, you enter the text between the brackets on the page. These brackets define the *text field.* A text field is simply an area in which you can enter text, graphics, or other items (such as an attached file). Depending on the document and the database template, you may see one or several fields. In some documents, a text field is preceded by a few words that explain the type of text you're to enter in the field. Figure 17.1 shows three types of fields: a text field, a rich text field, and a keyword field.

The following list describes the common fields and elements you'll find in Notes' database documents. Note that not all documents contain all of these elements.

- **Text Fields** Fields in which you can enter words and sentences, usually titles or topics.
- **Rich Text Fields** Fields in which you can enter text, import text, import graphics such as .PCX or .TIFF files, and attach files. The rich text fields usually make up the body of the document. (For more information about importing and attaching, see Lesson 9.)
- **Keyword Fields** Fields in which you can enter only specific words, such as categories, dates, or phone numbers. Depending on the database design, you may be allowed to enter your own keywords as well.

- **Time/Date Fields** Most often, these fields are automatically filled by Notes using your computer's clock. You may not be allowed to edit some time/date fields.
- **Number Fields** Fields that can contain only numbers, such as currency or quantities.
- **Document Author Field** A field that contains the document author's name. You cannot change the contents of this field.

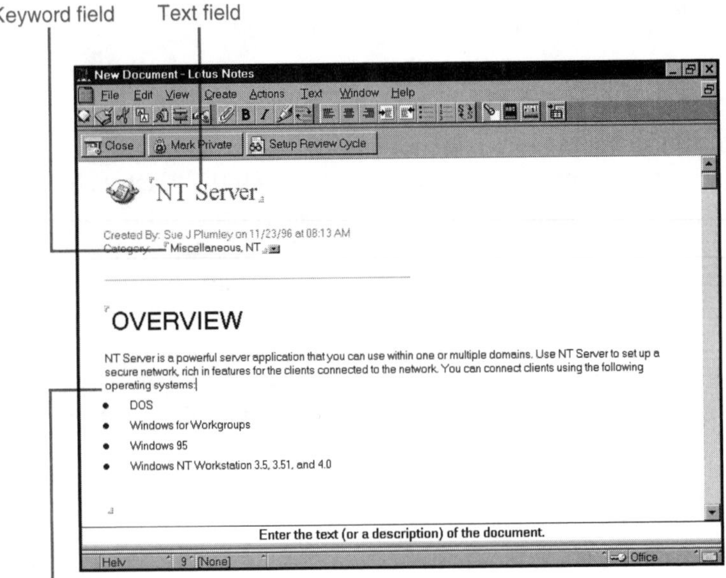

FIGURE 17.1 Use fields to enter text and graphics into a document.

Using Fields You cannot type anywhere in a Notes document that does not contain brackets. You must click within the brackets to add or edit text.

MOVING IN A DOCUMENT

You can move around in a document by using the scroll bars and mouse or by using the keyboard. You'll probably learn to use a combination of the two methods to get around in a document quickly and efficiently.

To use the mouse to move around a document, you use scroll bars. Lotus Notes displays a scroll bar along the right side and bottom of the document window when the document is too large to fit in the window. Within the scroll bar is the scroll box. The scroll box indicates the relative location of your insertion point within the document. Figure 17.2 shows a window with a scroll bar.

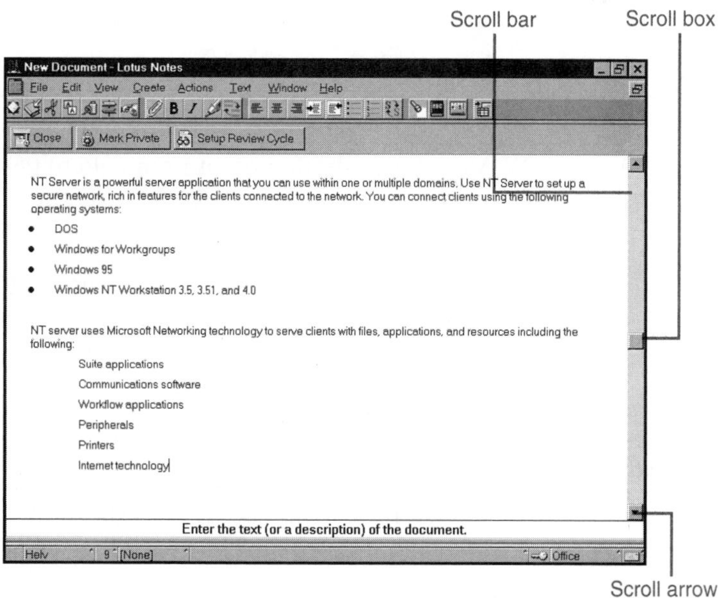

FIGURE 17.2 Use the scroll bar to quickly move around in a document.

When you scroll to any area in the document, you must click in that location before you can select, edit, or create text in that area. If you do not click to reposition the insertion point, the insertion point remains in its previous location. Use the following methods to scroll through a document:

- Click the up or down scroll arrow to move one line up or down in a document.
- Click the scroll box and drag it along the scroll bar to move up or down in a document more quickly.
- Click anywhere in the scroll bar to move to another location in the document.

As I mentioned earlier, you can also move around the document using your keyboard. Table 17.1 lists some keyboard shortcuts you can use.

TABLE 17.1 KEYBOARD SHORTCUTS FOR MOVING IN A DOCUMENT

SHORTCUT	RESULT
Tab key	Moves the insertion point from field to field (unless you're in a rich text field and then it inserts a tab).
Arrow keys	Moves the insertion point from character to character, line of text to line; when you reach the end of a field, the down or right arrow moves you to the next field.
Page Up/ Page Down	Moves the insertion point one screen at a time in the document.
Home	Moves the insertion point to the beginning of the current line of text.
End	Moves the insertion point to the end of the current line of text.
Ctrl+Home	Moves the insertion point to the beginning of the document (the first text field).
Ctrl+End	Moves the insertion point to the end of the document.

SELECTING TEXT

Before you can copy, move, delete, or format text in a document, you must select it. The quickest and easiest method of selecting text in a document is to click and drag the mouse I-beam across the text you want to select. When text is selected, it appears in reverse video as shown in Figure 17.3.

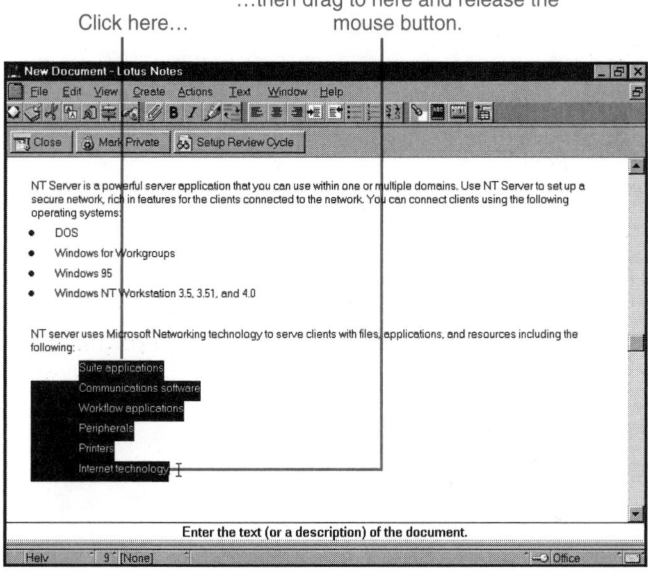

FIGURE 17.3 Click and drag the mouse to quickly select text.

Deselect Text If you selected too much text or you didn't mean to select text at all, click the mouse anywhere in the document to deselect the text. Alternatively, you can press the right or left arrow on the keyboard.

Shortcut Double-click any single word to select just that one word.

MOVING AND COPYING TEXT

You can move text from one part of the document to another or from one document to another. You also can copy text between documents or within the same document. Follow these steps to copy or move text.

1. Select the text you want to move or copy.
2. Choose Edit, Cut if you want to move the text, or choose Edit, Copy if you want to make a duplicate of the text. Notes moves or copies the text to the Clipboard.
3. Reposition the cursor where you want to place the text (it can be in the same document or in another document).

Window Menu If you want to place the cut or copied text in another document, use the Window menu to switch back to the database or to another open document.

4. Choose Edit, Paste, and the copied or cut text appears at the insertion point.

Shortcuts If you prefer to work from the keyboard, press Ctrl+X to cut text, Ctrl+C to copy text, and Ctrl+V to paste text.

UNDOING CHANGES

You often can undo editing or formatting changes you've made to a document. Undoing a change cancels the effects and returns the document to its previous state. For example, if you cut some text and you didn't mean to, you can undo that action. Notes simply puts the text back in its original location. To undo changes, choose Edit, Undo or press Ctrl+Z.

You must choose to undo an action before you perform another. Because Notes can remember only one action at a time, each new action replaces the last one.

Can't Undo Not all changes and edits can be undone. If the Undo command is dimmed, you cannot undo your previous command.

In this lesson, you learned to use text fields, move around in a document, select text, move and copy text, and undo actions. In the next lesson, you'll learn to format text and pages by changing fonts, setting alignment, and using page breaks.

LESSON

18 Formatting Text and Pages

In this lesson, you learn to change fonts, set spacing and alignment, use page breaks, and add headers and footers to a document.

Character Formatting

In Notes, you can change character formatting in any of the documents you create. Using character formatting, you can make your documents more interesting and attractive or you can emphasize important text. Character formatting includes working with all of the following characteristics:

- **Font** Apply a *typeface* to text in the document. For example, you can make a title stand out by assigning it a font different from that of all other text. And you can set the tone of the document or make body text easier to read simply by choosing certain fonts.
- **Type Size** Apply a size (say, 24-*point* size) to the text so titles are large and easy to read, and less important text is smaller (10-point, for example).
- **Attributes** Apply emphasis to text by making it bold or italic.
- **Styles** Apply preformatted characteristics (such as *bulleted text* or headlines) for quick and easy formatting.

Figure 18.1 shows a document that contains examples of each character formatting trait.

Font / Typeface A font is a style of type applied to text; Times New Roman, Courier, and Helvetica are common fonts.

Point A measurement of type; there are 72 points in an inch. Body text is generally 10- or 12-point, and headlines or titles are usually 14-, 18-, or 24-point.

Bulleted Text Text, usually in list form, that is preceded by a small black dot, an arrow, a check mark, or another item that makes the text stand out.

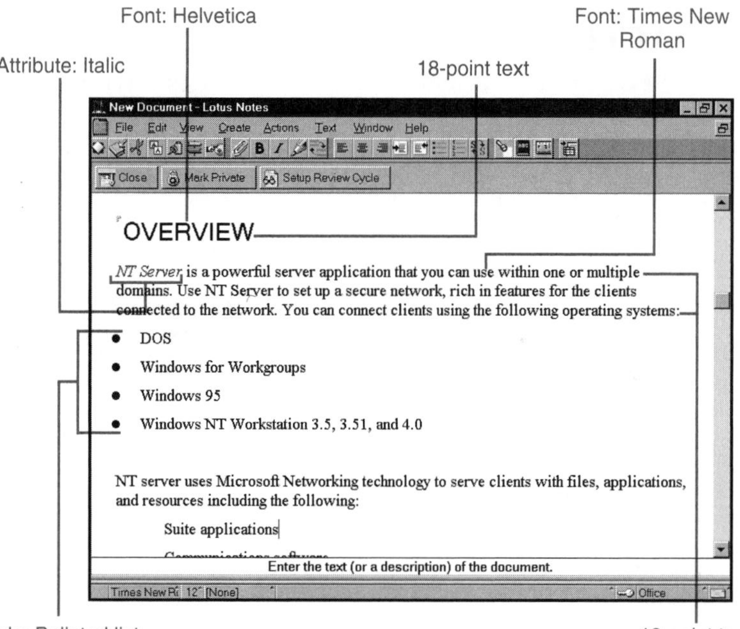

FIGURE 18.1 Make your documents more attractive with character formatting.

FORMATTING TEXT

To format text, follow these steps:

1. Select the text you want to format (as explained in Lesson 17).
2. Use the following methods to apply any text formatting you want:

   Font On the Status bar, click the Font button. A popup menu appears, listing the fonts that are available on your system. Select the font you want to use.

   Size On the Status bar, click the Type Size button and choose the point size you want from the popup menu shown in Figure 18.2.

   Style Click the Style button and choose the style you want to assign to the selected text.

   Attributes Click the Bold or Italic SmartIcon to apply the corresponding attribute.

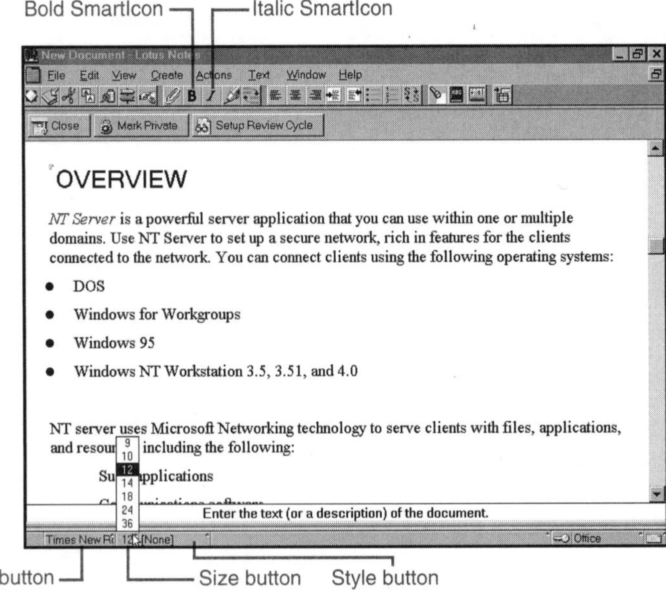

FIGURE 18.2 Use the Notes tools to format characters.

Alternative Method You also can set font, type size, and attributes using the Font tab in the Properties for Text InfoBox. To display the InfoBox, right-click the text and choose Text Properties from the shortcut menu. The Font tab is the first tab (the one showing when you open the InfoBox). To learn more about the Properties InfoBox, see the next section.

SETTING SPACING AND ALIGNMENT

You can adjust the spacing between lines of text in a document and the alignment of text in a document using the Properties for Text InfoBox. To display the InfoBox, right-click the text you want to align and choose Text Properties. The Properties for InfoBox appears. To use the spacing and alignment features (shown in Figure 18.3), click on the second tab in the InfoBox. For more information about InfoBoxes, refer to Lesson 3.

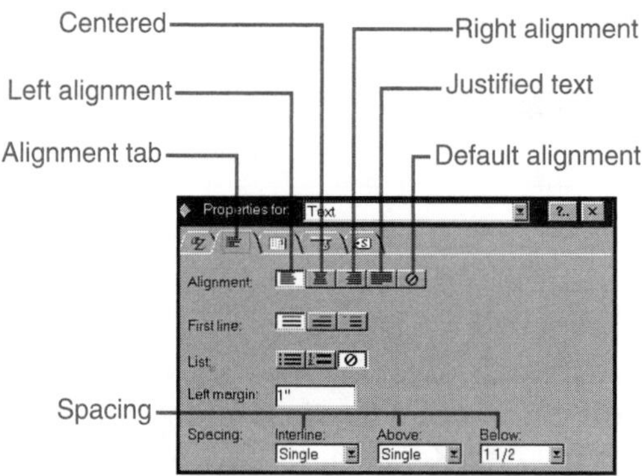

FIGURE 18.3 The Properties for InfoBox provides tools for governing how text in a paragraph looks.

To set alignment, select the text and click the appropriate alignment button. Left-aligned text has a flush left edge and a ragged right edge. Center-aligned text is arranged so that the distance from the left and right margins to the edge of the text is the same. Right-aligned text is text with a flush right edge and a ragged left. Justified text is text with flush left and right edges.

To set spacing, select the text and then choose from one of the following:

- Interline Determines the space between the lines of text in a paragraph.
- Above Determines extra space added above a paragraph.
- Below Determines extra space added below a paragraph.
- Single, 1 1/2, or double Sets the spacing for the selected paragraph.

Paragraph In Notes, a paragraph is defined as a line with a hard paragraph return (which you create by pressing Enter) at the end of it. A paragraph may contain several sentences, several words, or one word or letter, or it may even be a blank line.

USING PAGE BREAKS

Notes automatically breaks pages for you, but you might not always like where the page break falls. You can insert page breaks to organize the pages in your document to suit yourself.

Can't See Breaks? If you cannot see the page breaks that Notes creates, choose View, Show, Page Breaks.

To insert a page break, follow these steps:

1. Position the insertion point where you want a page break.
2. Choose Create, Page Break. Notes displays a thin black line across the page to show the page break (see Figure 18.4).

Page break

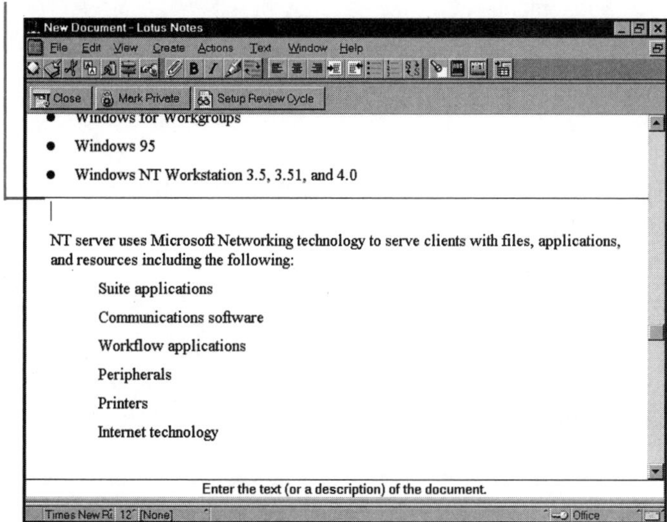

FIGURE 18.4 Separate pages for organization and printing purposes.

ADDING HEADERS AND FOOTERS

You use the Properties for Document InfoBox to insert page *headers* or *footers*. Headers and footers appear on the document only when it's printed.

Headers and Footers A header appears in the top margin of every page of the document, and a footer appears in the bottom margin of every page. Headers and footers often include such information as the creation date, author, title, page number, or company name. You can include any information you want to add to the document.

Follow these steps to add a header and/or a footer to your Notes document:

1. In the document, right-click the page and choose Document Properties from the shortcut menu.

No Document Properties? If Document Properties does not appear on the shortcut menu but Text Properties does, choose Text Properties. When the InfoBox opens, click the drop-down arrow in the title bar and choose Document.

2. Select the printer tab in the InfoBox (see Figure 18.5).

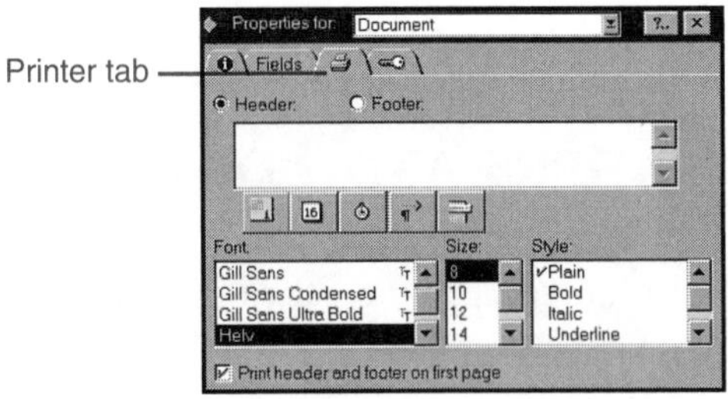

FIGURE 18.5 Header and footer options appear on the printer tab because they appear only in a printed document.

3. Choose Header or Footer. (You can always enter one and then come back and choose the other if you want to use both a header and a footer in your document.)

4. In the text box, enter any text you want in the header or footer, or click an icon below the text box to insert one of the following items:

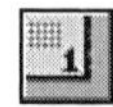

Page Number Inserts a symbol representing the page number; Notes replaces the symbol with the correct page number when the document is printed.

Date Inserts a field that displays the date of the day you print the document.

Time Inserts a field that displays the time you print the document.

Tab Sets a right tab in the header or footer.

Title Adds the document title to the header or footer.

5. In the Font, Size, and Style list boxes, choose the formatting for the header or footer.

6. (Optional) Choose the Print header and footer on first page check box.

7. Close the InfoBox and then save the document.

8. To view the header or footer, print the document by choosing File, Print and clicking OK in the File Print dialog box.

Print? For more information about printing, see Lesson 6.

Figure 18.6 shows a header printed on the first page of a document. The date and the document title appear in the header.

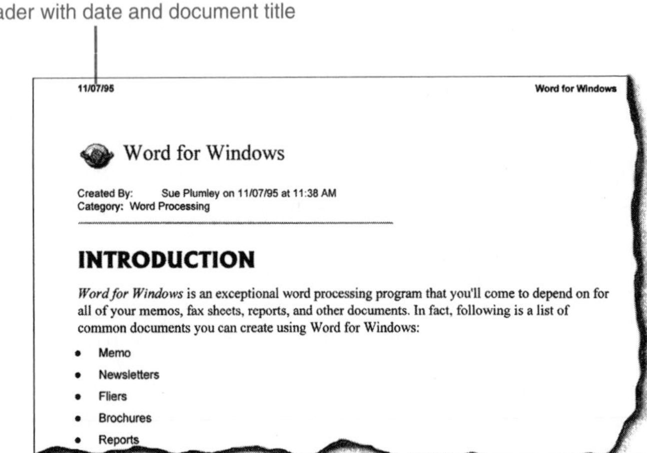

FIGURE 18.6 Insert any information you want in the header or footer of a document.

In this lesson, you learned to change font characteristics, set spacing and alignment, use page breaks, and create headers and footers in a document. In the next lesson, you'll learn to create, edit, and format tables.

LESSON 19

Using Tables

In this lesson, you learn to create, edit, and format tables in your documents.

Creating Tables

You can create *tables* to organize the data in a document. After you create a table in Notes, you enter data into cells, which are the intersections of the table's columns and rows. The data in a table might be words, phrases, or numbers.

Table One or more organized list of data presented in columns and rows. A table can only appear in a rich text field (see Lesson 17).

To create a table, follow these steps:

1. In the document, position the insertion point in a rich text field and choose Create, Table. The Create Table dialog box appears (see Figure 19.1).

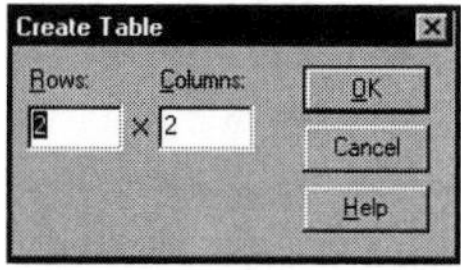

Figure 19.1 Enter the number of rows and columns.

2. In Rows, enter the number of rows you want in your table. In Columns, enter the number of columns. (You can change these numbers later if necessary.)

3. Click OK to create the table. In your document, Notes inserts a grid with the number of columns and rows you specified. In addition, it adds the Table menu to your menu bar, as shown in Figure 19.2.

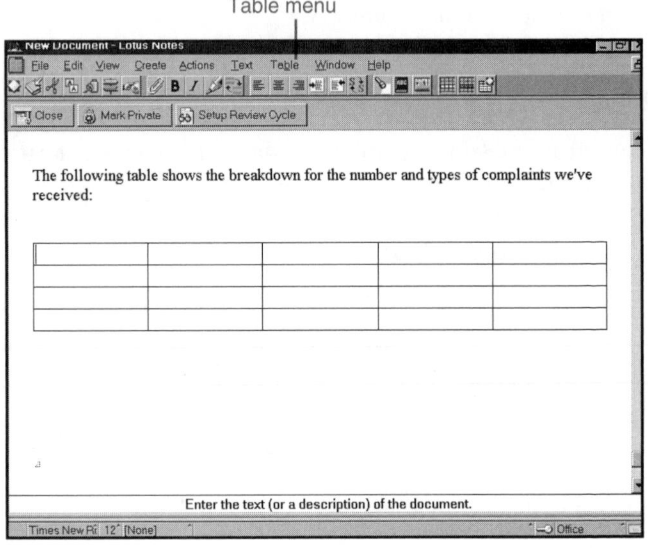

FIGURE 19.2 A table grid helps you organize your data.

ENTERING DATA IN A TABLE

To enter data in a table, you place your insertion point in any cell and begin typing. If you continue to type past the end of the cell, Notes wraps the text within the cell as you type, adjusting the cell height to accommodate the text. Use the Backspace and Delete keys to edit the text in the table, just as you would any other text in a document.

To move around a table, you can click in any cell you want to move to. If you prefer, you can also use any of the following keyboard keys:

- **Tab** Moves the insertion point to the next cell to the right. At the end of a row, the insertion point moves to the first cell in the next row.
- **Shift+Tab** Moves the insertion point to the previous cell.
- **Arrow keys** If the cells are empty, the left and right arrow keys move the insertion point to the next cell in that direction. If the cells contain data, the left and right arrow keys move through the data one character at a time and then to the next cell. The up and down arrow keys always move from row to row.

Selecting Table Text You select text in a table just as you would any text in a document—by dragging the mouse across the text.

EDITING TABLES

You can edit the table, and you can edit the text within a table. You edit text in a table as you would any text. For example, you can select the text and then delete it, you can insert new text, and you can copy and paste the text.

Another important feature enables you to edit the table itself by adding and deleting rows and columns. To add rows or columns, follow these steps:

1. Position the insertion point in the row above which you want to insert a new row, or in the column immediately to the right of where you want to insert a new column.
2. Choose Table, Insert Row or Insert Column. Notes inserts the row or column in the table. Figure 19.3 shows a table with an added row and column.

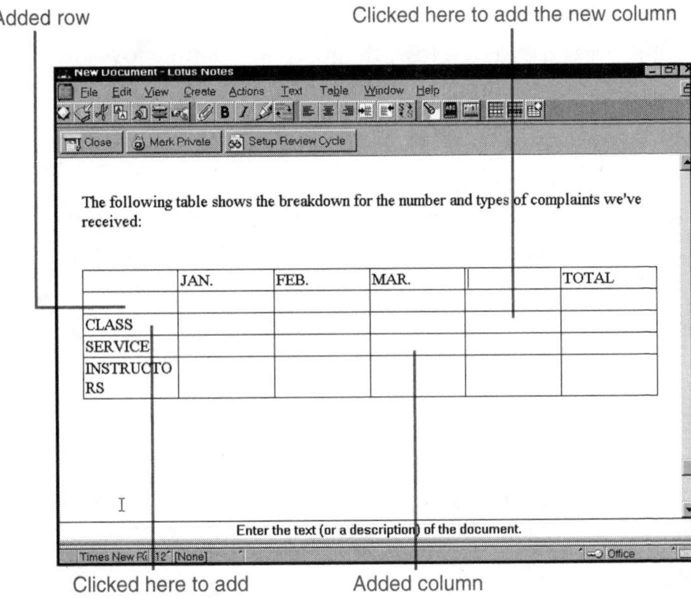

FIGURE 19.3 Notes inserts the row or column in front of the insertion point.

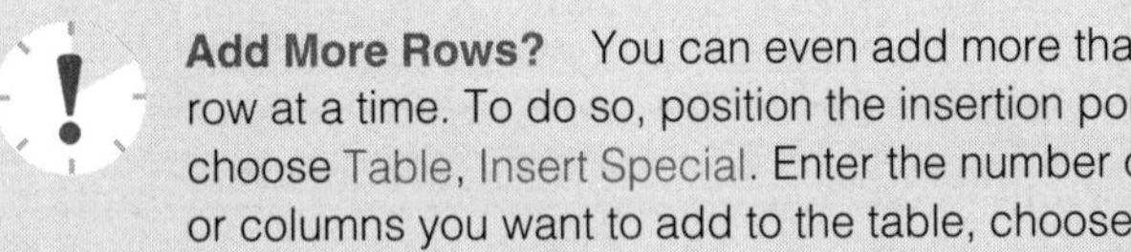

Add More Rows? You can even add more than one row at a time. To do so, position the insertion point and choose Table, Insert Special. Enter the number of rows or columns you want to add to the table, choose Row or Column, and choose Insert.

The following steps show you how to delete a row or column:

1. Position the insertion point in the row or column you want to delete.
2. Choose Table, Delete Selected Row[s] or Delete Selected Column[s]. A confirmation dialog box appears.
3. Click Yes to delete the row or column.

Delete More To delete more than one row or column, choose Table, Delete Special. Then enter the number of rows or columns, choose Row or Column, and click the Delete button. Click Yes to confirm the deletion.

To quickly add one row or column at the end of the table, choose Table, Append Row or Append Column. Or you can simply place your insertion point in the last cell in the table (the intersection of the last column and the last row) and press the Tab key.

FORMATTING TABLES

After you enter your data, you can format both the text within a table and the table itself. To format text in a table, select the text and apply formatting using the Text menu commands or the Status bar buttons. (Lesson 18 covers formatting text in a document.)

By default, the table itself is formatted with a single line outlining the table and separating the columns and rows. To modify that, you can select certain cells or the entire table, and you can remove all borders or add a double border.

To format the table, follow these steps:

1. Double-click the table to put it in *edit mode*. Then right-click in the table and choose Table Properties from the shortcut menu. The Properties for Table InfoBox appears (see Figure 19.4).

Edit Mode Edit mode means the document is ready to accept text.

2. Select the cells to which you want to apply a border.
3. Select the type of border you want to apply to the selected cells. Extruded and embossed add a bit of variety to the standard border.

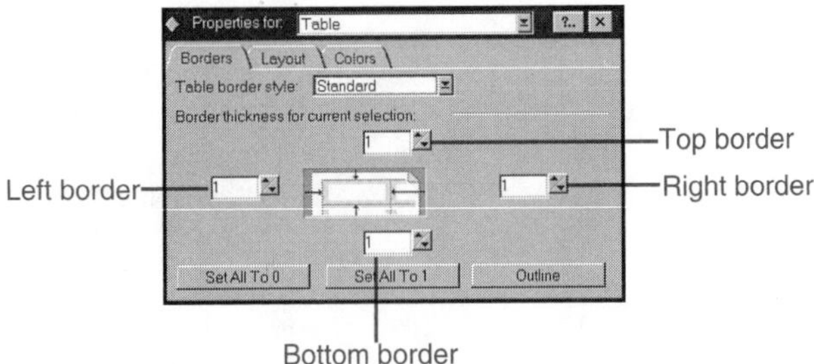

FIGURE 19.4 Use the Properties InfoBox to apply cell borders.

Figure 19.5 shows a table with a standard border applied to the entire table.

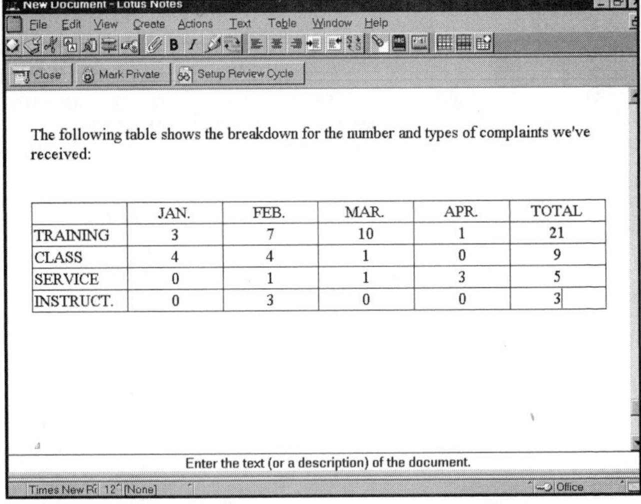

	JAN.	FEB.	MAR.	APR.	TOTAL
TRAINING	3	7	10	1	21
CLASS	4	4	1	0	9
SERVICE	0	1	1	3	5
INSTRUCT.	0	3	0	0	3

FIGURE 19.5 Apply a heavy outline to make the table stand out.

In this lesson, you learned to create a table, enter text in the table cells, edit data, and format the table and its cells. In the next lesson, you will learn to find and replace text in a document. After reading the next lesson, you will also be able to find specific text in a database.

Finding and Replacing Text

LESSON 20

In this lesson, you learn to find text in a document, replace that text, and find text in a database.

Finding Text in a Document

You can easily find words or phrases in a document in Notes. You might want to find specific text in order to read about a topic, to refer to the page on which it appears, or to replace that text with new text.

To find specific text in a document, follow these steps:

1. With the document in edit mode, choose Edit, Find/Replace. The Find and Replace dialog box appears (see Figure 20.1).

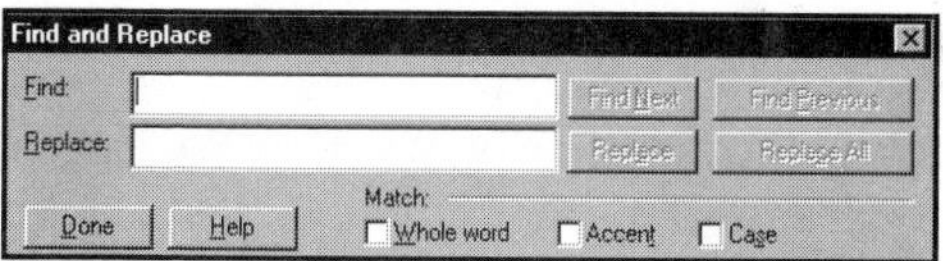

Figure 20.1 You can find all occurrences of a word or phrase in your document.

2. In the Find text box, enter the text you want to find. The entry can consist of up to 45 characters and spaces, depending on the characters you enter and whether or not you use capital letters.
3. (Optional) In the Match area of the dialog box, choose any of the following options:

Whole Word Finds the character string you entered only when a space precedes and follows the word. For example, if you enter "the" and do not choose Whole Word, Notes finds such words as "their," "there," "other."

Accent Tells Notes to include diacritical accent marks (such as those that are used in foreign languages).

Case Searches for the character string that matches the case exactly, such as with names of programs or people.

4. Click the Find Next button to find the next occurrence of the word in the text. Choose the Find Previous button to find the previous occurrence of the word. If it finds a match, Notes highlights the word in the text and leaves the Find and Replace dialog box open.

5. If you just wanted to locate the word, click the Done button to close the dialog box so you can work in the document. If you want to replace the found word, move on to the next section. Figure 20.2 shows the Find and Replace dialog box, as well as the highlighted word that Notes found in the document.

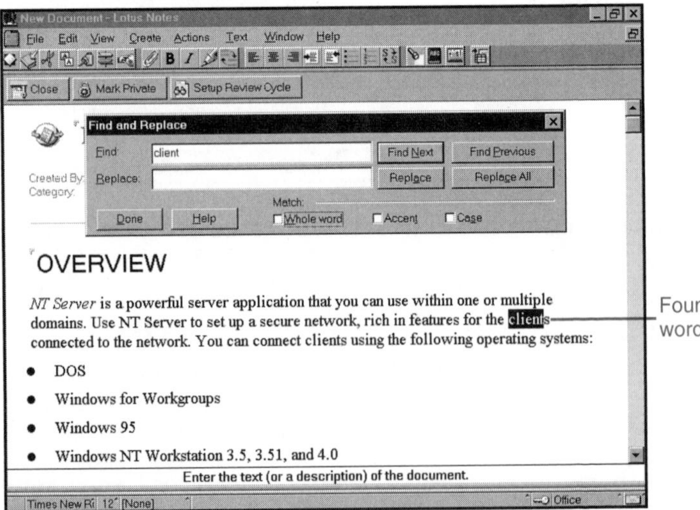

FIGURE 20.2 You can find words anywhere in the document.

Shortcut Press Ctrl+G to find the word or phrase again without opening the Find and Replace dialog box. Notes remembers what you entered in the Find and Replace dialog box the last time, and it finds that text again.

REPLACING FOUND TEXT

After you find text, you can replace it quickly and effortlessly using the Find and Replace dialog box. Follow these steps to replace the found text:

1. In edit mode, choose Edit, Find/Replace. The Find and Replace dialog box appears.
2. In the Find text box, enter the text you want to locate.
3. (Optional) In the Replace text box, enter the text you want to substitute for the found text.
4. Choose any options you want to apply.
5. Click the Find Next or Find Previous button to move to the first occurrence of the word or phrase in the respective direction. If Notes finds a match, it highlights the text.
6. (Optional) Click the Replace button to replace the highlighted text that Notes found with the text you typed in the Replace text box. Or if you're sure you want to replace all occurrences, click the Replace All button to replace them all automatically.
7. (Optional) Click Find Next or Find Previous to skip this occurrence and find the next occurrence of the specified text.
8. When you finish with the Find and Replace dialog box, click Done.

Careful! Before you choose to Replace All in the Find and Replace dialog box, save your document in case something goes wrong. If you make a mistake, close the document without saving it. Then open it and try again.

FINDING TEXT IN A DATABASE

Notes even enables you to search through any database of documents for specific words or phrases without opening each document. Instead of using the Find command, you use the Search bar. Notes searches the entire database and lists all documents containing the specified word or phrase.

To search through an entire database, follow these steps:

1. In database view, choose View, Search Bar. The Search bar appears below the SmartIcon bar in your database.
2. Enter a word or phrase in the Search for text box.
3. Click the Search button. Notes lists all the documents that contain the word or phrase, with a check mark beside each one (see Figure 20.3).
4. Click the Reset button to start a new search and display all of the documents in the database.

You can also set search criteria when you use the Search bar. To do so, click the button at the right end of the Search bar. The popup menu shown in Figure 20.4 appears.

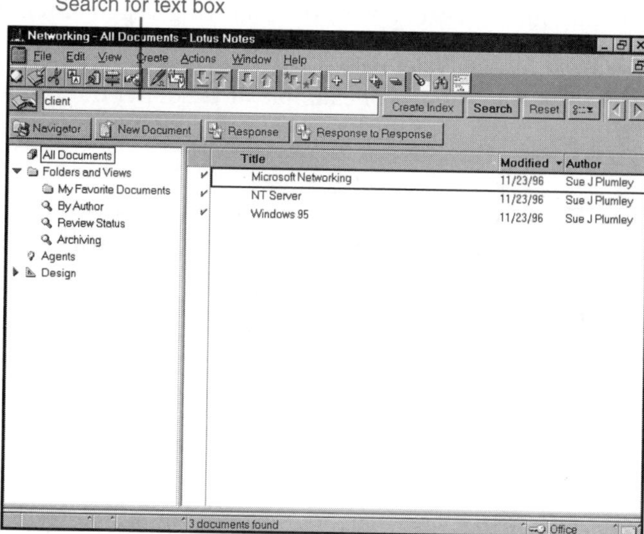

FIGURE 20.3 Notes lists the documents that contain the search text.

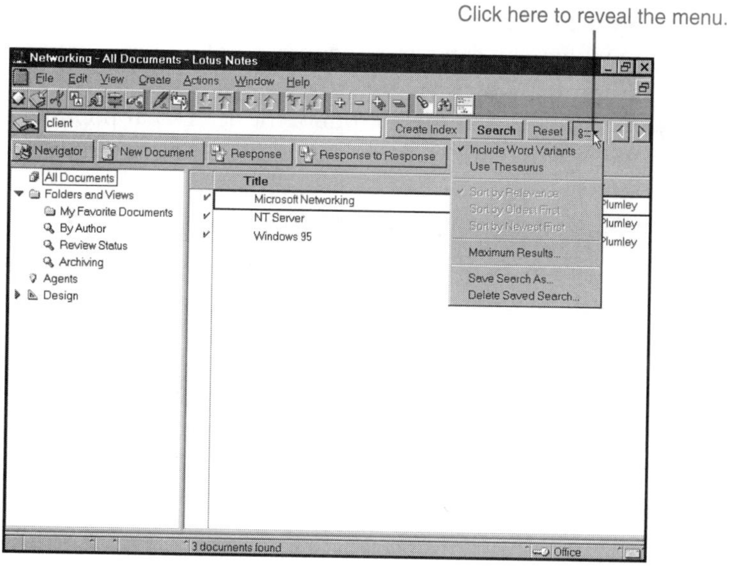

Click here to reveal the menu.

FIGURE 20.4 Set search criteria using the Search bar popup menu.

In the popup menu, select any of the following search criteria:

- **Include Word Variants** Includes such variants as plurals in the search. For example, if you enter the word "network," Notes finds "networks," "networking," and so on.
- **Use Thesaurus** Includes synonyms in the search string; for example, if you're searching for the word "test" and you choose to Use Thesaurus, Notes searches for other words such as "quiz."
- **Sort by Relevance** Lists the documents with the most occurrences of the word first.
- **Sort by Oldest First** and **Sort by Newest First** Sorts the documents by date.
- **Maximum Results** Displays the Maximum Results dialog box in which you enter the maximum number of finds you want Notes to display; the default is 250 documents.
- **Save Search As** Displays the Save Search As dialog box in which you can name the search so that you can use it again with other databases. Once you save a search, its name appears at the bottom of the Search bar popup menu. Select the name to automatically carry out the search.
- **Delete Saved Search** Displays the Delete Saved Search dialog box from which you select saved searches and delete those you no longer use.

In this lesson, you learned to find and replace text within a document and to search for text in a database. In the next lesson, you learn to use the spell checker, doclinks, and popups.

Using Advanced Editing Techniques

In this lesson, you learn to check your spelling, reference other pages with doclinks, and add information for the reader in popups.

Checking Spelling

Notes provides a spell checker that you can use to make sure your documents are presentable to others on the network. To check your spelling, follow these steps:

1. With your document in edit mode, choose Edit, Check Spelling. Notes begins the spell check. If Notes finds a questionable word, it highlights the word and displays the Spell Check dialog box shown in Figure 21.1.

You're in Luck! If Notes does not find any misspellings, it displays a message that says **No Misspellings Found**. Click OK to continue editing your document.

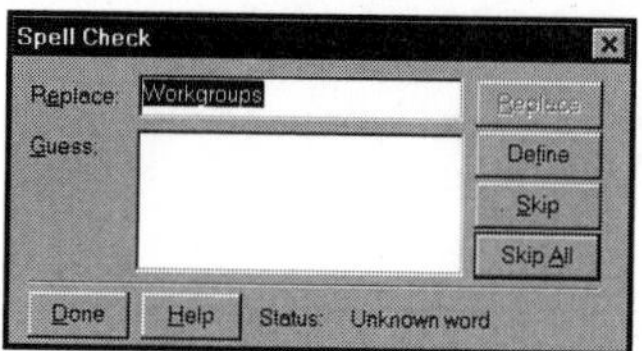

Figure 21.1 Notes displays any questionable words or spellings.

2. In the Spell Check dialog box, use one of the following techniques to tell Notes what to do about the word in question:

   Type the correct spelling in the Replace text box and click Replace.

   Select the correct spelling from the Guess list box and click Replace.

   Click the Define button to add the word to the dictionary so Notes doesn't question the spelling again.

   Click the Skip button to ignore this particular occurrence of the word.

   Click Skip All to ignore all occurrences of this word in this document.

   Click Done to quit the spell check.

3. If you choose any of the previous options except Done, Notes carries out your command and continues to check the spelling. Repeat step 2 for each word Notes stops on.

4. When Notes completes the spelling check, it displays the message shown in Figure 21.2. Click OK to close the spell checker.

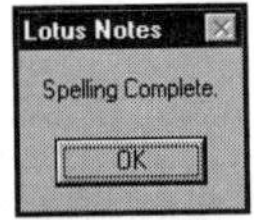

FIGURE 21.2 Notes tells you when it finishes the spell check.

REFERENCING DOCUMENTS

Sometimes you'll find that several of your documents contain related information and the reader would benefit from viewing both documents. You can include a reference, or *doclink*, to one document within another document. Then by double-clicking the doclink, the reader can open and view the second document. You can add doclinks to documents within the same database or in different databases.

To reference a document, follow these steps:

1. Place the insertion point in the document *to* which you want to refer the reader.
2. Choose Edit, Copy As Link. Choose the type of link you want to copy and Notes copies the text to the Clipboard.

Link The word "link" comes from the longer "hyperlink," a term used in programming long before Windows. Both refer to a live connection between two or more documents. When documents have a live connection and the text in the source document changes, the linked text in the destination document is automatically updated to reflect the change.

3. Open the document in which you want to create the doclink.

Document Switch To switch to another document, open the Window menu, choose the name of the database, and open the second document. (Or you can select the name of the document from the Window menu if the document is already open.)

4. In edit mode, position the insertion point where you want to add the doclink and choose Edit, Paste. Notes inserts the doclink icon, a small page with the corner turned down (see Figure 21.3).
5. (Optional) If necessary, add text to tell the reader how to open the doclink.

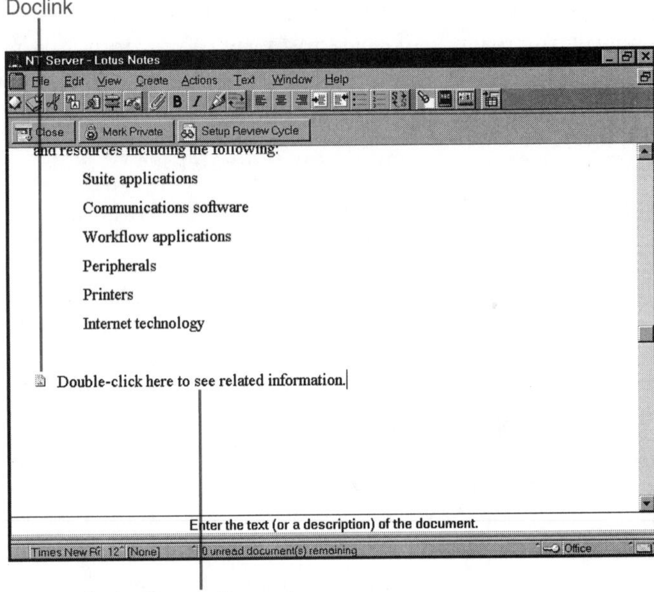

FIGURE 21.3 A doclink gives the reader quick access to related information.

> **Delete Doclink** You can delete a doclink by positioning the insertion point in front of the document icon and pressing the Delete key. You cannot undo a doclink deletion, but you can paste the link again.

To open a doclink within a document, just double-click the doclink icon. The second document opens immediately. When you finish reading it, choose File, Close to return to the original document.

ADDING DEFINITIONS AND EXPLANATIONS

Suppose you've placed a proposal document in a network database, and you want to provide an explanation of a process you mentioned that you don't know if everyone on the network will know about. You can add extra information—such as a definition or an explanation of text—to a document by using what Notes calls a *popup*. Popups are brief messages that appear when the reader clicks on a marked area of text. Figure 21.4 shows a text popup in a document.

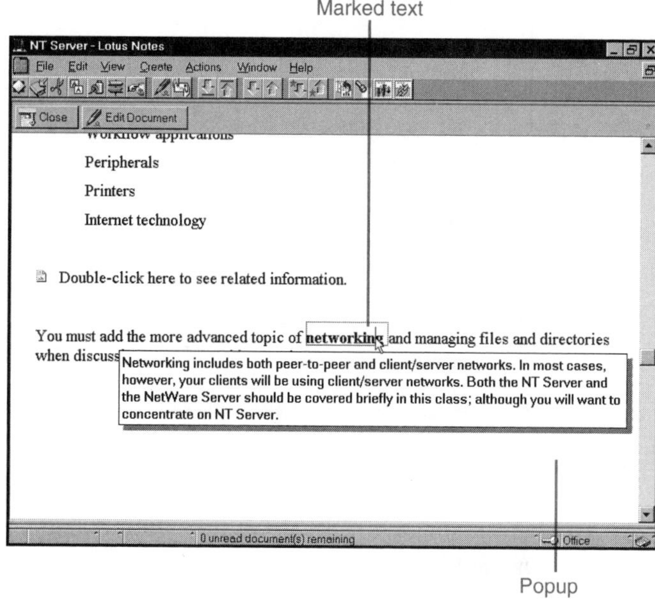

FIGURE 21.4 Add information and interest to your documents with popups.

Follow these steps to add a popup to your document:

1. In edit mode, select the text you want to define or explain.
2. Choose Create, Hotspot, Text Popup. The Properties for HotSpot Popup InfoBox appears (see Figure 21.5).
3. In the Popup text box, enter the text that you want Notes to display when the reader clicks on the marked text. (The text can exceed the window's size limit.)

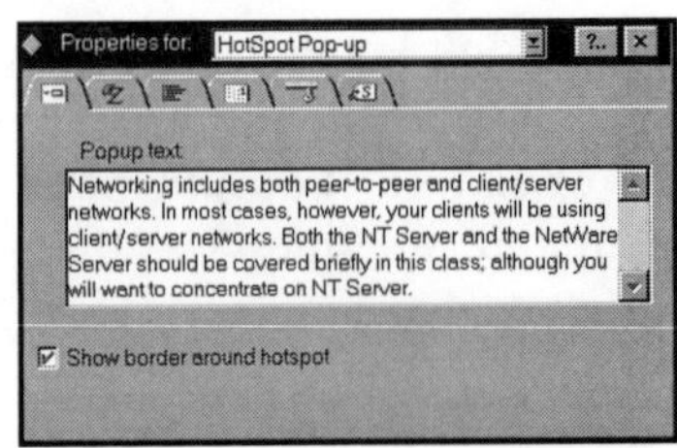

FIGURE 21.5 Enter a description or explanation.

4. (Optional) If you want to mark the selected text, select the Font tab (the second tab in the InfoBox), and you'll see the options shown in Figure 21.6. Choose a different font, size, style, and/or color.

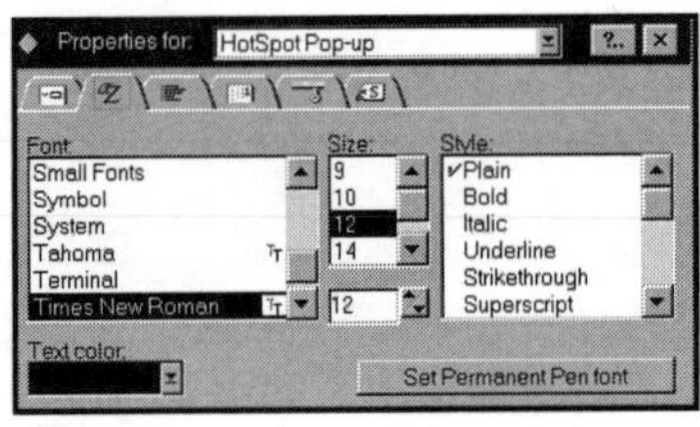

FIGURE 21.6 Change the selected text to make it stand out.

5. When you are done, close the InfoBox by clicking the Close (X) button. To view the popup, you must save the document, close it, and then reopen it so that it's not in edit mode.

To view a popup, the reader clicks on the marked text. The popup remains on-screen as long as the reader holds the mouse button.

In this lesson, you learned to check your spelling, create a doclink reference, and add a text popup to a document. In the next lesson, you will learn to manage document groups.

Configuring for Calendaring and Scheduling

In this lesson, you learn to set options for your calendar profile, choose who may view your calendar, and change view options.

What Is Calendaring and Scheduling?

You use calendaring and scheduling to keep track of appointments, check the calendar of other Notes users, and invite co-workers to meetings and appointments. The calendar, which is part of your mail database, enables you to do the following:

- Schedule appointments on your own calendar
- Schedule meetings and invite others to those meetings
- Enter repeating appointments, such as a weekly or monthly meeting
- View the free time of mail users who may use Notes mail, Office Vision, or cc:Mail
- View your appointments by the day, week, or month

CALENDAR VIEWS

You can view your calendar and the information it contains in two different views.

- **Calendar View** This view displays appointments and meeting information in a two day, one week, two week, or one month format.

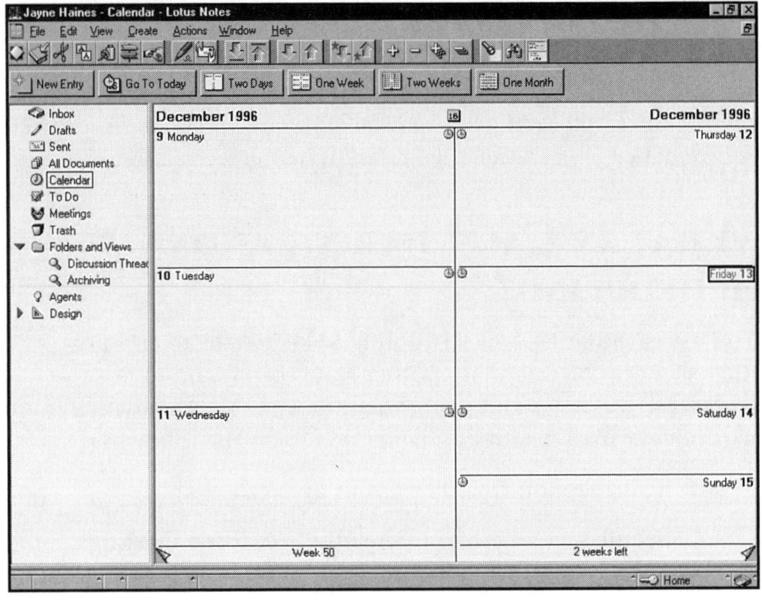

FIGURE 22.1 View your appointments by the week.

- **Meetings View** This view lists meeting invitations and meetings you have accepted by date and meeting time.

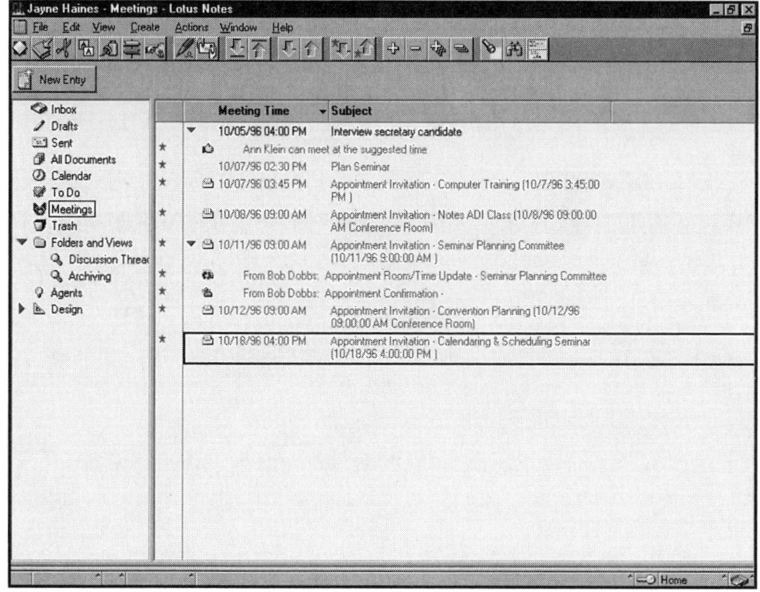

FIGURE 22.2 View meetings in a list format.

SETTING OPTIONS

You use two documents contained in your mail database to administer your calendaring and scheduling functions:

- **The Calendar Profile** lets you set defaults for the appointment alarm and free times.
- **The Delegation Profile** enables you to choose who can read your calendar, open your mail, send mail on your behalf, and delete mail in your mail database.

SETTING THE CALENDAR PROFILE

Your Notes Adminstrator may have completed your Calendar Profile document for you; however, if she didn't, you can set the profile yourself. If you click the calendar view and receive a message that your Profile must be set, follow the steps below. You also can use the steps below to confirm the settings in your profile. Figure 22.3 shows the Calendar Profile document with the default settings.

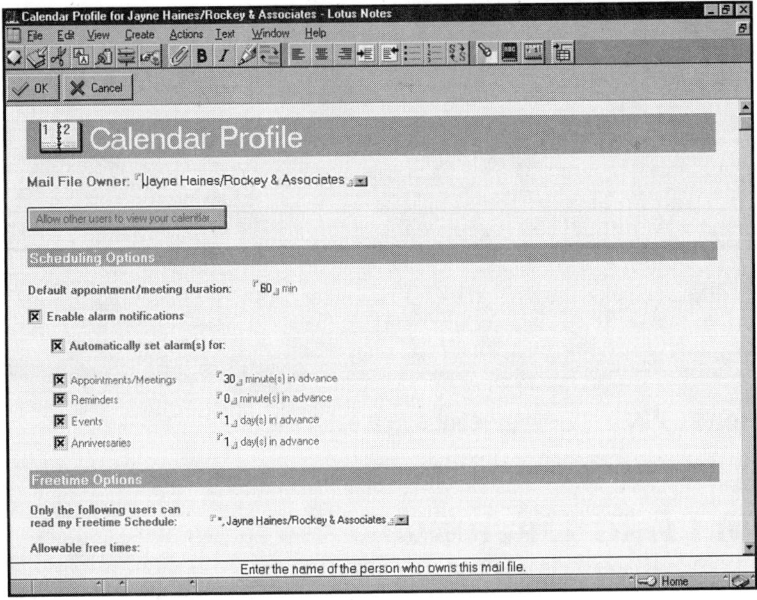

FIGURE 22.3 Change the defaults in the Calendar Profile document.

To configure your Calendar Profile, follow these steps:

1. Open your mail database.
2. Choose Actions, Calendar Tools, Calendar Profile from the menu. Confirm that your name appears in the Calendar Owner field of the document.
3. If you want to enable others to view your calendar, you can click the text **Click Here to Allow Other Users to**

View Your Calendar. This will open the Delegation Profile, which is covered in the next section, "Setting the Delegation Profile."

4. In Scheduling Options, enter a time limit as a default for appointment durations. You also can check the Enable the Alarm Daemon check box if you want Notes to warn you prior to any meetings or appointments.

Daemon Pronounced "demon," a program that automatically runs in the background, collecting information or performing operating system administration tasks.

5. In Freetime Options, enter the names of the people you want to have access to your calendar by clicking in the Freetime Schedule field; alternatively, you can click the down arrow beside the option and choose names from your address book.

6. Use the list of Allowable Free Times to set the days and hours available to others to view.

7. You can set Notes to add meeting invitations to your calendar automatically. Click the Advanced Calendar Options and click the Meetings check box in Autoprocessing Options. You can also choose to remove invitations from your inbox after you respond to them.

8. In the Calendar Entry Options area of the document, set options for conflict checking and default viewing settings.

9. Choose the OK button on the Action Bar to save the settings and close the document. You can also choose the Cancel button to cancel all changes you made to the document and close it.

SETTING THE DELEGATION PROFILE

The Delegation Profile lets you specify the people who may read your mail and view your calendar. You can also specify that the designated people can send messages and replies on your behalf or can delete any of your mail documents. Figure 22.4 shows the Delegation Profile document. You can open the Delegation Profile by clicking the text **Click here to allow other users to view your calendar** in the Calendar Profile document.

Delete My Mail? Reply to My Messages? No Way! Be careful when you enable others to send mail on your behalf or to delete your mail from your mail file. These privileges should be reserved for only those you trust implicitly.

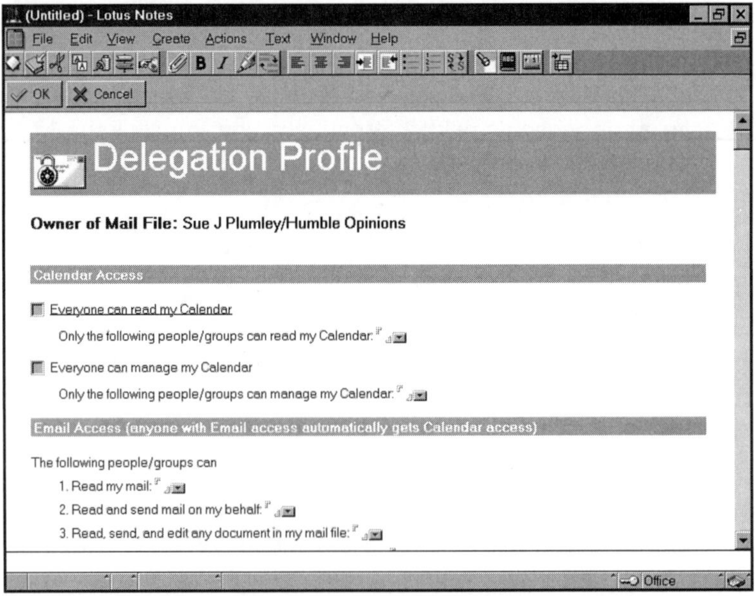

FIGURE 22.4 The Delegation Profile. Specify who may access your mail and calendar.

To edit the Delegation Profile document, follow these steps:

1. Open your mail database.
2. Open the Actions, Calendar Tools menu and choose Calendar Profile.

3. Click Click Here to Allow Other Users to View Your Calendar. The Delegation Profile document appears.
4. In Calendar Access, choose either or both of the following options:

   Everyone Can Read My Calendar Enables others to view your calendar but not make changes or additions to it.

   Everyone Can Manage My Calendar Enables specified people to add, delete, and edit your calendar entries.

   You can enter the names of the people to whom you grant permission to view your mail database, or you can click the down arrow and choose names from the address book.
5. In Email Access, choose or enter the people to whom you want to give access to your mail for each of the following options:

   Read My Mail Gives the designated people the right to only read your mail messages.

   Read and Send Mail on My Behalf Enables the designated people to read all of your mail and to reply or send new messages with your name as the sender.

   Read, Send, and Edit Any Document in My Mail File Gives the right to read and send mail, as well as to edit messages, attachments, imported documents, and so on in your mail file.

   Delete Mail Use this option in conjunction with options 2 and 3, enabling the designated user to delete any of your mail messages.

E-mail Access Means Calendar Access Notice that if you grant a person or group access to your e-mail, you're also granting them access to your calendar, since your calendar is in your mail database.

6. Click the OK button in the action bar to save the changes and close the document; click the Cancel button to cancel the changes and close the document. Click OK again to close the Calendar Profile document.

CHANGING VIEW OPTIONS

The Calendar is one view in your mail database, just like Inbox, Drafts, To Do, Meetings, and other views. To view the calendar, open your mail database and click on the Calendar. Figure 22.5 shows a one week view of a calendar.

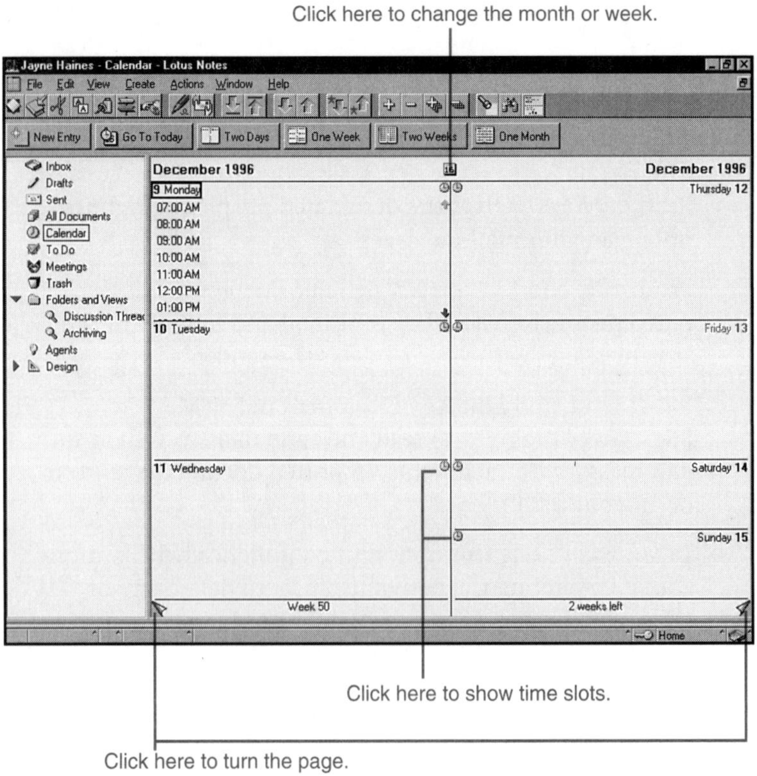

Click here to change the month or week.

Click here to show time slots.

Click here to turn the page.

FIGURE 22.5 Enter appointments and meetings in your calendar.

Do the following to change the view of the calendar:

- To turn a page in the calendar, click the curl at the bottom of the page.
- Click the small clock icon in the corner of any day to display the time slots. Alternatively, choose View, Calendar, Show Time Slots.
- Click the date icon in the middle of the calendar's title bar to change the month, week, or day.
- Click one of the following buttons, in the action bar, to change the Calendar's view: Go To Today, Two Days, One Week, Two Weeks, or One Month.
- Choose View, Calendar, and Go To; enter a specific date in the text box and choose OK.
- You also can view meetings from your mail database. Choose the Meetings view to see appointments listed by time, date, and subject.

In this lesson, you learned to set options for your calendar profile, choose who may view your calendar, and change view options. In the next lesson, you will learn how to use the calendar.

LESSON 23

Using the Calendar

In this lesson, you learn to make calendar entries, invite people to meetings, and to respond to invitations.

Making Calendar Entries

When you make a calendar entry, you're creating an appointment, event, reminder, or other item that will appear in your calendar. The calendar entry appears on the specified date and at the time you defined. Besides the date and time, you can enter other details about the entry, as described in the following list:

- Choose from the following as an entry type: Appointment, Invitation, Event, Reminder, or Anniversary.

Appointment—Schedule any appointment you want by entering a brief or long description, date, and time, and set options for public viewing.

Invitation—Use an invitation when you want to schedule a meeting to which you invite others. You enter a description, time, date, and then enter or choose the people you want to invite.

Event—An event usually lasts one or more full days, as opposed to the hour setting used in a standard appointment. You also can add a brief or detailed description and a date.

Reminder—A reminder is similar to an appointment: you enter a description, date, and time to enter in to your calendar.

Anniversary—An anniversary usually occurs once a week, month, or year and will be entered into your calen-

- **Date**—Enter the date of the calendar entry; or click the month button to view the month and select a date.
- **Time**—Set the duration of the calendar entry by setting a beginning and ending time in the Time text box; some appointment types enable you to enter a beginning time only. You can, alternatively, click the clock button to view the time scale; drag the indicators up or down on the scale to set the time and duration of the appointment. Time doesn't appear in an Anniversary or an Event.
- **Brief description**—Enter a brief description of the entry, such as a person's name or the topic of the meeting.
- **Detailed description**—Enter names, places, topics, or any other text in this field to create a detailed description of the calendar entry.
- **Room**—Enter the room in which the meeting will take place; this is available only with the Invitation calendar entry.
- **Not for Public Viewing**—Click this check box if you do not want others to see the appointment in your calendar.
- **Pencil In**—Click this check box to show the appointment or meeting is tentative.

Figure 23.1 shows the New Appointment document for an invitation. Many of the fields and options change when you choose a different calendar entry type.

You can create a calendar entry by following these steps:

1. To create a calendar entry, open your mail database and choose the Calendar view. Do one of the following:

- Click the New Entry button on the Action Bar.
- Choose Create, Calendar Entry.
- Double-click on the day you wish to create an entry for in the calendar.

2. Choose the entry type you want to create: Appointment, Invitation, Event, Reminder, or Anniversary.

3. Enter a description, the date, time, and any other details or options you want.

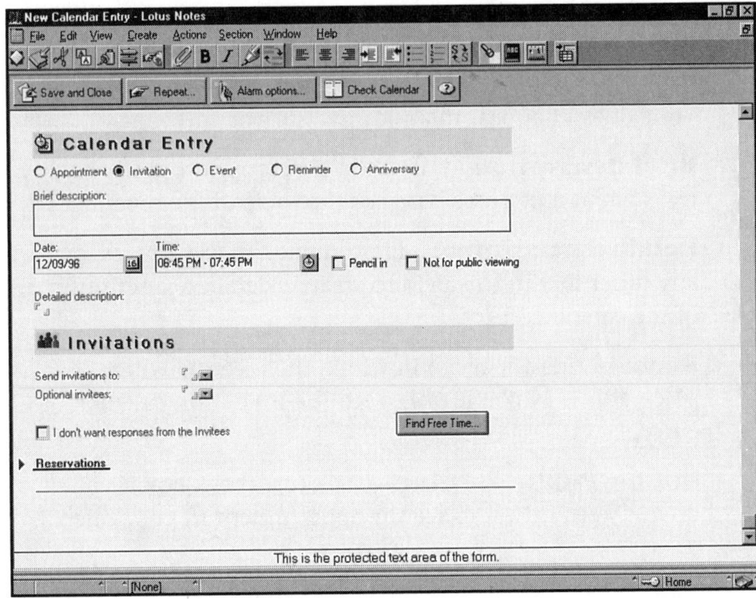

FIGURE 23.1 Create an invitation to a meeting using Notes Calendar feature.

4. To create a repeated entry, click the Repeat button on the Action Bar. The Repeat Rules dialog box appears. Select the days, dates, and any other repeating options and choose OK to return to the Calendar Entry document.

5. To set an alarm, click the Alarm Options button on the Action Bar. If you haven't enabled alarms in your Calendar Profile, a dialog box appears and asks if you want to do that now; choose Yes.

6. In the Set Alarm dialog box, choose whether to sound the alarm before, after, or on the specified time; if you choose before or after, enter the number of minutes the alarm will ring before or after the entry time. Choose OK.
7. Choose the Save and Close button to close the entry and enter it into your calendar.

INVITING OTHERS TO MEETINGS

You can create an appointment or meeting in your calendar, called an Invitation, and invite others to attend. Notes creates the invitations and e-mails them to all invitees, listing the date, time, and duration of the meeting as well as a description. You also can check the free time of the invitees, if you want to choose a meeting time that's convenient for all.

To invite others to a meeting, follow these steps:

1. Create a new entry that is an Invitation. Enter the date, time, description, and other details (refer to the previous section).
2. Click the Send Invitations To down arrow in the Invitations area of the document and choose the names from the address book; alternatively, enter the names in the provided field. You can choose from the following:

   Send Invitations to—Enter the names of those you require to attend.

   Optional Invitees—Enter the names of those who may attend the meeting if they want to.
3. To view the free time of the invitees, click the Click here to find free time for all invitees. The Free Time dialog box appears, as shown in Figure 23.2.

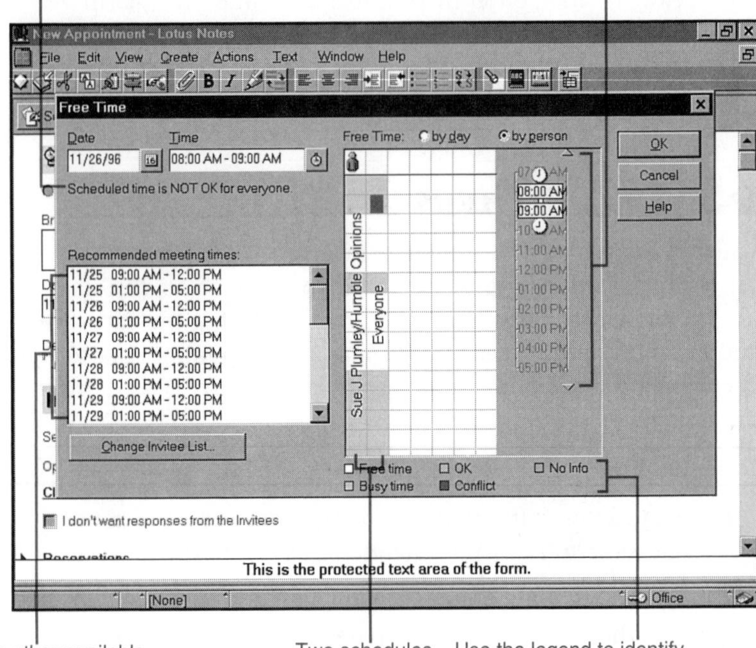

FIGURE 23.2 Check to see if your invitees can attend your meeting.

What if Schedules Aren't Available?—If an invitee's schedule isn't available to you (the free time is kept in a separate database on the server), that person has not enabled you to see his/her schedule or you are working remotely. The best thing to do in this case is to send the invitation and ask for a response.

4. Check the individual schedules in the Free Time window to the right of the dialog box. You can check either by day or by person.

5. You can change the date and time, and even the people you've invited to the meeting, in the Free Time dialog box.

6. Choose OK when you're finished with scheduling around the free time.

7. Click the Save and Close button to save the appointment. Notes displays a dialog box asking if you want to send invitations; choose Yes.

After you send the invitations, your appointment appears on your calendar. You can view or edit the appointment at any time by double-clicking the appointment.

No Response From an Invitee?—Invitees do not have to respond to your messages; however, if an invitee is not using Notes, cc:Mail, or Office Vision, he or she cannot respond. You can only send invitations to others on the Notes network.

RESPONDING TO INVITATIONS

When you receive an invitation from someone, it appears as a mail message in your Inbox. The subject begins with Invitation, so it's easy to find. You can open the message and respond to it through Notes e-mail.

To respond to an invitation, follow these steps:

1. In your Inbox, open the Invitation. Notes displays the Invitation document (as shown in Figure 23.3).

Who Else is Invited?—Click the Invitees option at the bottom of the Meeting Invitation document to see who else has been invited to the meeting.

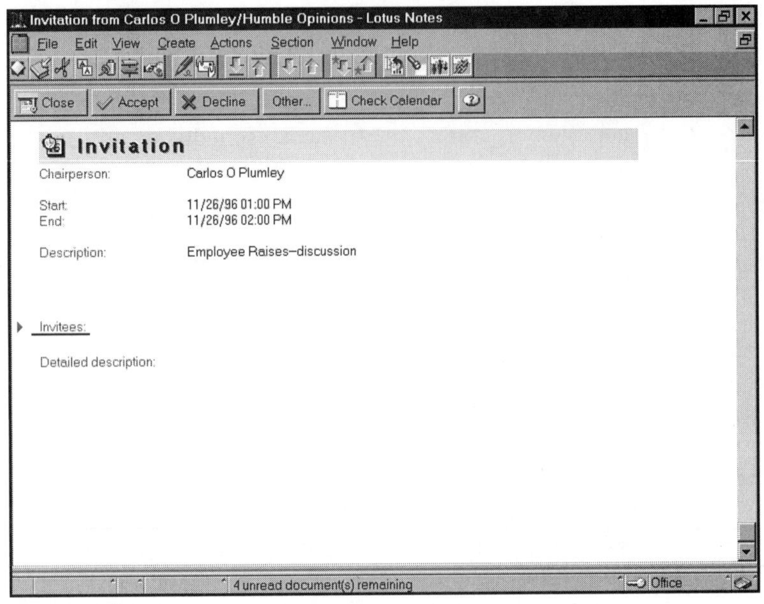

FIGURE 23.3 View the meeting invitation and then respond.

2. Choose one of the following options from the Action Bar:

   Close—Closes the invitation without further action.

   Accept—Sends a message saying you will attend the meeting.

   Decline—Sends a message saying you cannot attend the meeting.

   Other—Displays the Options dialog box from which you can choose the following options: Accept, Decline, Delegate, or Propose Alternative Time/Location. Select one and choose OK.

   If you choose to Delegate the meeting, the Delegate To dialog box appears; enter the person's name to whom you want to delegate the meeting and choose OK.

If you choose the Propose Alternate Time/Location option, Notes adds a section to the message called "Proposed Change." Enter the reason for the change, proposed date and time, and/or proposed time. Click the Send Counter Proposal button on the Action Bar and Notes sends the message for you.

If you choose Check Calendar, Notes displays your calendar so you can check your schedule before you reply. Press Escape to return to the Invitation and respond.

3. After you select an option, Notes displays the appropriate Status dialog box informing you of its next action, such as sending your acceptance of the invitation. Notes then closes the Invitation and returns to your mail database.

In this lesson, you learn to make calendar entries, invite people to meetings, and to respond to invitations. In the next lesson, you will learn to customize Notes.

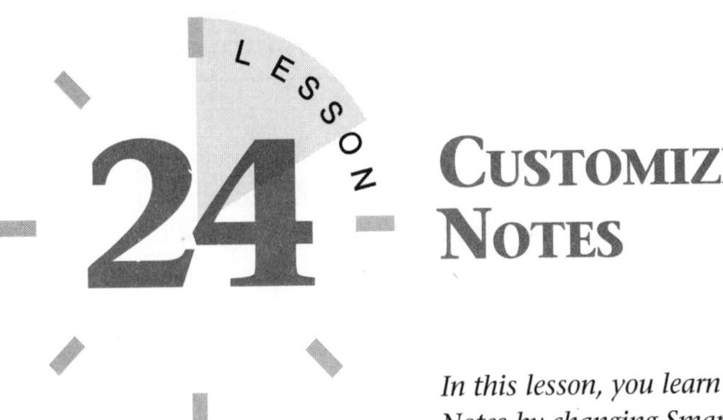

Customizing Notes

In this lesson, you learn to customize Notes by changing SmartIcons, arranging workspace pages, changing mail setup, and setting user location.

Changing SmartIcons

In Notes, you can use SmartIcons as shortcuts for common tasks and commands. However, you might find that you don't often use the SmartIcons that Notes displays by default. You can modify the SmartIcon bar to include whichever SmartIcons you prefer. To change the displayed SmartIcons, follow these steps:

1. In your workspace, choose File, Tools, SmartIcons. The SmartIcons dialog box appears (see Figure 24.1). The list on the left shows all available icons; the list on the right shows the icons in the bar that's currently displayed.

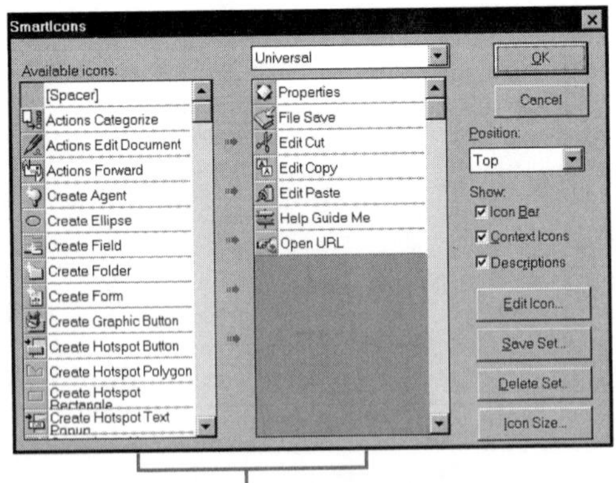

Figure 24.1 Modify the current SmartIcon bar or create your own bar.

2. To add an icon to the selected icon bar, drag it from the list of Available icons to the list on the right. To remove an icon from the list on the right, drag it to the list on the left.

Don't Like the Order? You can move icons around in the icon list on the right. Simply drag each icon to the desired location.

3. When you finish adding and rearranging icons, click Save Set to save the changes you made to the icon bar. The Save Set of SmartIcons dialog box appears (see Figure 24.2).

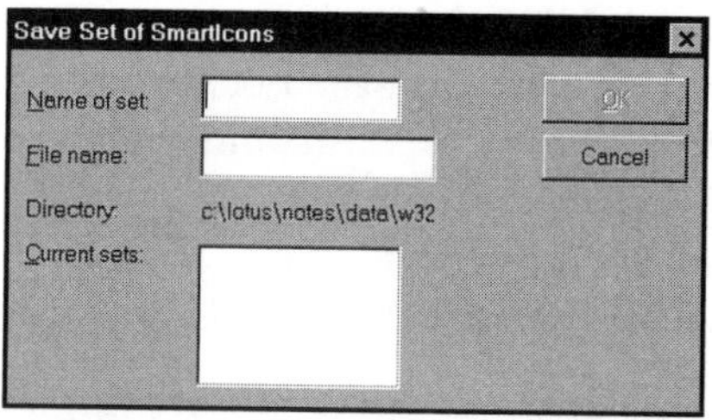

FIGURE 24.2 Save the set of SmartIcons so you can use it anytime.

4. In the Name of set text box, enter a brief descriptive name.
5. In the File name text box, enter a name for the icon file. Use eight characters or fewer, and add the .SMI extension for ease in file management.
6. Click OK to close the Save Set of SmartIcons dialog box. The new SmartIcon bar appears in the drop-down list of SmartIcon bars above the list on the right. You can choose to display this icon bar or any other.

7. In that top drop-down list, choose the icon bar you want to display and click OK. Notes displays the selected icon bar in the workspace.

Change Positions You can change the position of the SmartIcon bar, moving it to the left, right, or bottom of the Notes workspace. To do so, open the Position drop-down list in the SmartIcons dialog box and select a new location for the bar.

CHANGING USER PREFERENCES

Notes enables you to change a number of settings that affect your workspace and how you work in Notes. You can control such things as when Notes scans for unread documents, when it should prompt you to empty the trash, and whether it saves a copy of the mail you send. You'll find these options in the User Preferences dialog box (shown in Figure 24.3). To open the User Preferences dialog box, choose File, Tools, User Preferences.

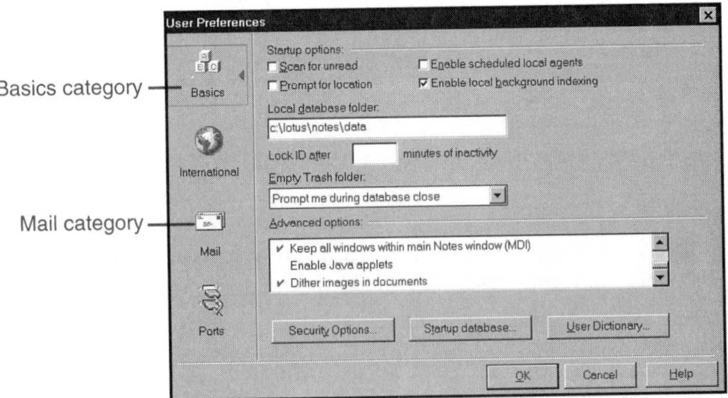

FIGURE 24.3 You might change the options in the Basics or the Mail category.

More Information This lesson covers only the common, most basic options you can customize in User Preferences. If you need more information about customizing User Preferences, see Que's *Special Edition Using Lotus Notes.*

Changing Basics Options

Click on the Basics icon to access the Basics category in the User Preferences dialog box (refer to Figure 24.3). There you can work with the following options: Startup options, Local database folder, Empty Trash folder, User Dictionary, and Advanced options. Table 24.1 describes the common settings for each of these areas.

Table 24.1 Basics Options

Option	Description
Startup options	Contains check boxes for commands you can have Notes perform automatically at startup. Choose the Scan for unread check box to indicate Notes should scan for unread mail and documents in selected databases on your workspace when you first start Notes. (For more information on scanning databases, see Lesson 13.)
Local database folder	Displays the path to the folder on your hard drive that holds your database files. You can change the path if you want to store your databases in another folder.

OPTION	DESCRIPTION
Empty Trash folder	Governs how Notes empties your trash folder. Choose whether you want to be prompted when you close the database, whether you always want it emptied when you close the database, or whether you want to empty it manually. (To learn more about using the trash folder, see Lesson 6.)
User Dictionary	Enables you to view words you've added to your User Dictionary during spell checking. You can add, update, and delete any of these words. (For more information about spell checking, see Lesson 21.)
Advanced options	Contains a list of options that control how you use Notes. A check mark appears beside active options. Click on an option to select or deselect it.

Scared of the Advanced Options? If you're unsure of an option's meaning, read about the option in Notes' Help system before you activate it. (Lesson 4 covers using the Help system in detail.) If you do check an option and you don't like the results, open the User Preferences dialog box and deselect it.

CHANGING MAIL OPTIONS

You can change Mail options by clicking on the Mail category icon in the User Preferences dialog box. Figure 24.4 shows the Mail options, and Table 24.2 describes them.

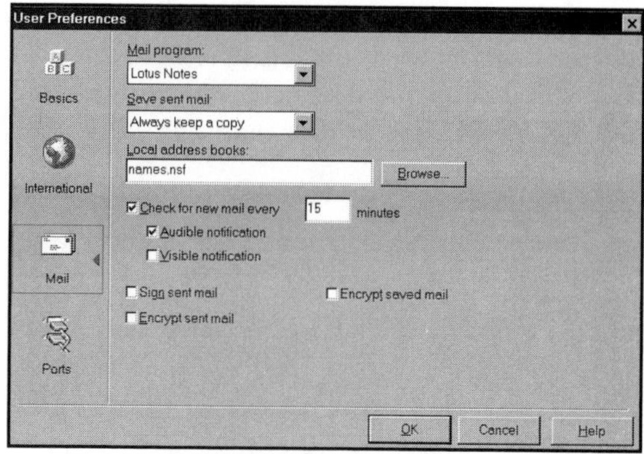

FIGURE 24.4 The options in the Mail category.

TABLE 24.2 MAIL OPTIONS

OPTION	DESCRIPTION
Mail program	Displays the name of the mail program you're using, such as Lotus Notes or cc:Mail.
Save sent mail	Controls whether Notes keeps a copy of the mail messages you send or prompts so you can decide which messages to keep a copy of.
Local address books	Lists the path and file name of your local address book. You can enter a new path and file name, or you can click the Browse button to search for another path.
Check for new mail every ___ minutes	Tells Notes how often to automatically check for new mail addressed to you.
Audible notification	Controls whether Notes sounds a beep or any other sound upon receipt of new mail.

OPTION	DESCRIPTION
Visible notification	Controls whether Notes displays a message in the Status bar upon receipt of new mail.
Sign sent mail	Tells Notes to always add your name, date, and time signature to your mail (see Lesson 8).
Encrypt sent mail	Tells Notes to always protect the mail you send so it can be opened only by the person to whom it's addressed (see Lesson 8).
Encrypt saved mail	Tells Notes to always protect the mail you save so others cannot view it.

When you finish changing settings in the User Preferences dialog box, click OK to close it.

CHANGING YOUR PASSWORD

Depending on how your Notes network is set up, you may be required to enter your password when you first log on to Notes, or you may have to enter a password only when you want to modify documents and databases. You can change your Notes password at any time to ensure that your mail and databases are safe from others in your company.

Follow these steps to change your password:

1. Choose File, Tools, User ID. Enter your password if prompted. The User ID dialog box appears (see Figure 24.5).
2. Click the Set Password button, and the Enter Password dialog box appears.
3. Enter your password. (A series of Xs appears in the text box to ensure your privacy.) Click OK, and the Set Password dialog box appears.

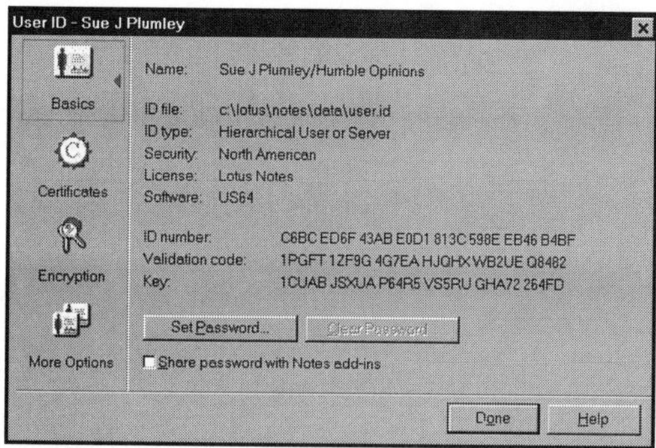

FIGURE 24.5 Change your password periodically to secure your system.

4. Enter your new password and click OK, and the Set Password confirmation dialog box appears.

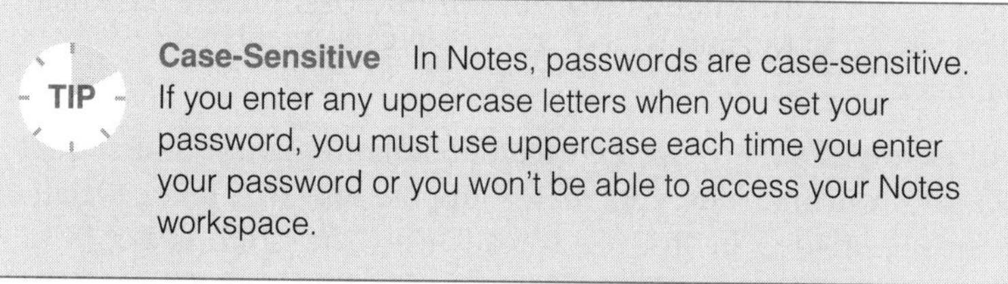
TIP

Case-Sensitive In Notes, passwords are case-sensitive. If you enter any uppercase letters when you set your password, you must use uppercase each time you enter your password or you won't be able to access your Notes workspace.

5. Enter your new password again and click OK to confirm it.
6. Click Done to close the dialog box.

In this lesson, you learned to change SmartIcon bars, user preferences, and your password. In the next lesson, you will learn to link and embed data in Notes.

LESSON 25

LINKING INFORMATION

In this lesson, you learn about linking and embedding data to your database documents.

UNDERSTANDING LINKING AND EMBEDDING

Most Windows applications enable object linking and embedding (OLE) between applications and between documents; Notes is no exception. You use linking and embedding as a method of sharing data between documents so you can save time in your work. You also use these features so that your data can quickly and easily be updated.

For example, suppose you create a document about the first quarter sales within a Notes database. Suppose also that you have all of your sales figures in an Excel spreadsheet. You can link a copy of the spreadsheet to the Notes document so that your readers can open the spreadsheet file and view your data. And as a bonus, if you choose to link the document, any changes you make in the Excel spreadsheet automatically update the link in your Notes document.

When you *link* data, you copy the data from one document or application (called the source), and you paste the data in a special way to another document or application (called the destination). A connection, or link, exists between the two documents so that any changes in the source are automatically updated in the destination.

When you *embed* data, you actually create one document within another. For example, you might want to place a picture in a Notes database document. In the Notes document, you open the graphics application (the source), create the picture, and then save the picture within the Notes document (the destination). Anytime you want to edit the picture, you double-click it, and the source application opens so you can edit the picture.

I Can't Edit! In order to edit data you've linked or embedded from another application to a Notes document, you must have the source application installed on your computer.

You can link and embed text, pictures, spreadsheets, tables, or sound and video clips, all of which are called *objects*. There are many advantages to linking and embedding objects. Linking saves disk space and makes use of objects you've already created and want to use again. In addition, linking enables you to use one source and many different destinations; and all destinations are automatically updated when you make changes to the source. Embedding, on the other hand, uses more disk space, but it makes editing the object within the document a quick and easy task. Embedding also enables you to change the object in the destination document without changing the source document.

LINKING DATA

In Lesson 21, you learned how to create a link (doclink) between documents within Notes. Now you learn to link data between Notes and another application.

To link data from another application to Notes, follow these steps:

1. In the source application, select the data you want to link and choose Edit, Copy (as shown in Figure 25.1). Windows copies the data to the Clipboard.
2. Using the Windows 95 taskbar or the Task List, switch to the Notes application and open the database and document to which you want to link the data.

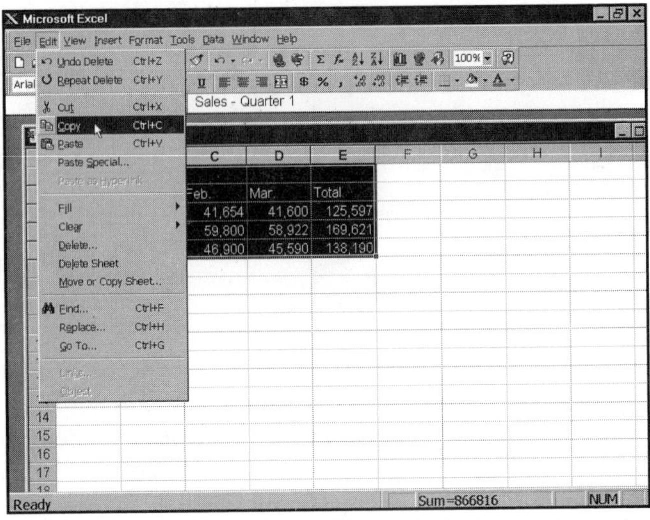

FIGURE 25.1 You can link data from Excel to a Notes document, for example.

3. Position the insertion point where you want the link and choose Edit, Paste Special. The Paste Special dialog box appears (see Figure 25.2).

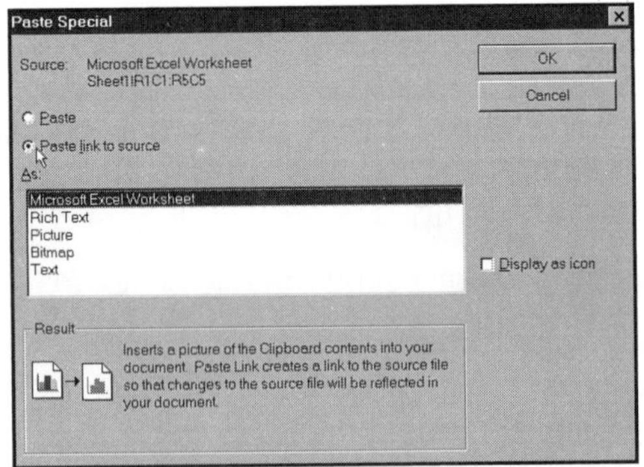

FIGURE 25.2 Paste the data on the Clipboard as a link in the Notes document.

4. Choose the Paste link to source option.
5. In the As list, select the type of data you're pasting (if it's not already selected).
6. Click OK to paste the data to the Notes document. Figure 25.3 shows an Excel table in a Notes document.

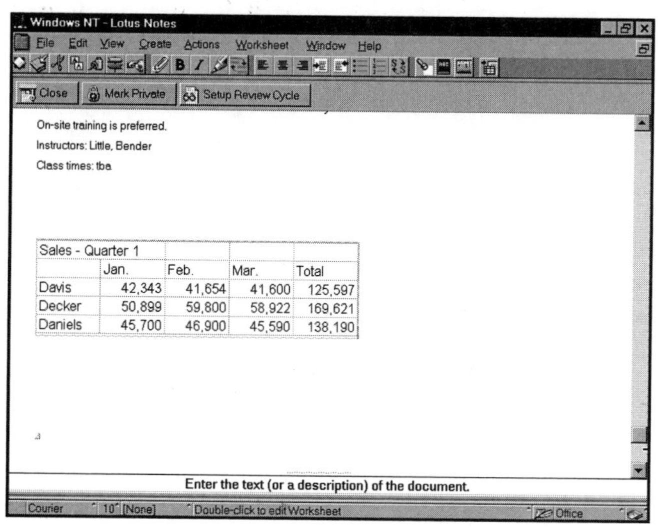

FIGURE 25.3 An Excel spreadsheet that's linked to a Notes document is automatically updated.

Quick Edit To edit a linked item, double-click it, and the source application opens with the data ready to edit. When you change data in the source application, the data automatically changes in the destination.

EMBEDDING DATA

When you embed data, you create an object—text, table, picture, or sound file—within the destination document. Embedding uses more disk space and more memory because when you create or change an embedded object in the destination document, you must actually open and use two programs at one time.

Follow these steps to embed data:

1. In edit mode, position the insertion point in the Notes document where you want to create the embedded object.
2. Choose Create, Object. The Create Object dialog box appears (see Figure 25.4).

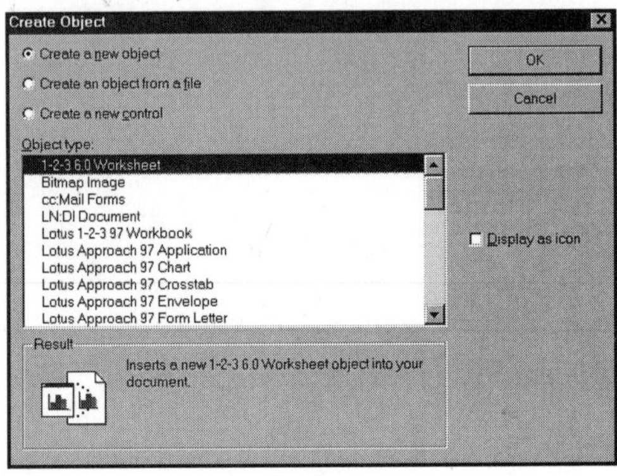

FIGURE 25.4 Choose the type of object you want to create.

3. Choose Create a new object if you want to create an object using one of the applications listed. Choose Create an object from a file if you want to embed an existing object.
4. In the Object type list, select the kind of object you want to add to the Notes document. (What types of objects you can create depends on the programs installed to your computer.)
5. Click OK, and the application opens within the Notes document with all the tools and menus you need to create the object. Figure 24.5 shows a Notes document with the Windows Paint program open, ready for the user to create an embedded object.

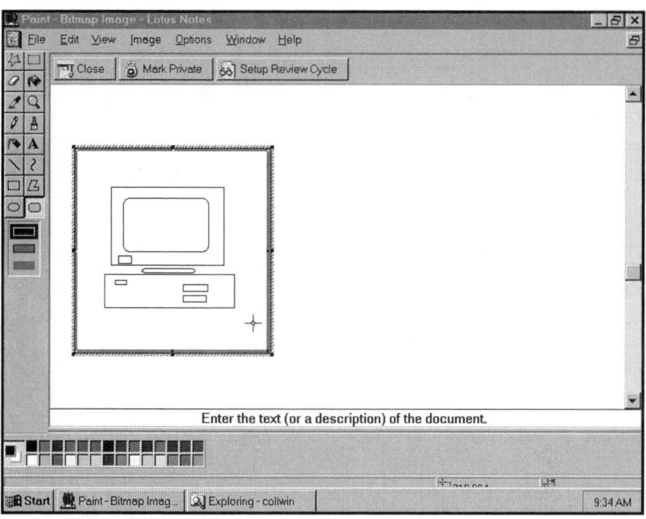

FIGURE 25.5 The Paint program is open within Notes.

6. When you finish creating the object, click anywhere in the Notes document outside of the object's *frame*. The source application closes, and the object appears in the Notes document (see Figure 24.6).

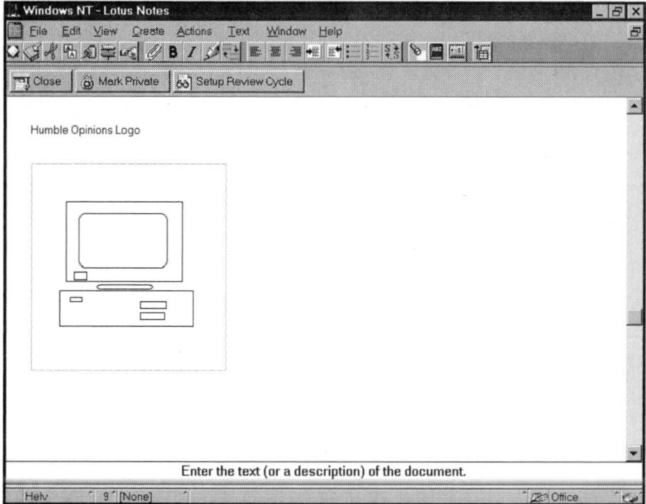

FIGURE 25.6 An embedded Paint object in a Notes document.

Frame The box that appears around many embedded or linked objects in a Notes document. You can usually click and drag the bottom right corner of the frame to resize the object within the document.

To edit any embedded object, double-click the object, and the source application opens. Edit the object as you want. When you finish, click outside the frame of the object to close the source application.

UPDATING LINKS

When you open a document that contains linked data, Notes displays a message asking if you want to refresh the links in that document. Click Yes to update the links and to update all data in the object. To update the changes in the Notes document at any other time, change to Edit mode and choose View, Refresh.

If you click No when you're asked to update a link, the links are broken. Once the links are broken, any changes made to the source are not updated in the destination document. You can still double-click the object and open the source application, but the changes you make there will not be updated in the destination.

Shortcut To refresh the view at any time—and thus update the links—press F9.

In this lesson, you learned to link data and embed data and to update links. In the next lesson, you learn to work remotely with Notes.

Working Remotely with Notes

LESSON 26

In this lesson, you learn how to set up a modem, how to connect to and disconnect from a network, and how to replicate mail and databases.

Understanding Remote Connections

Domino includes many features that help you connect remotely to your network by way of a modem instead of a direct cable. You use remote connections with Domino when you're working away from the office, at home, or on the road with a notebook computer. You can complete your work—mail, document creation, task lists, and so on—on your computer without being attached to the network. Then when you're ready, you call up the server and transfer the data from your Notes program to the network.

Before you plan to connect to the server remotely, check with your Domino administrator to make sure you have a certified Domino User ID and appropriate access to the Domino server. You also need to make sure that the server is set up to receive incoming calls through a modem. Finally, you should know the exact name of your server.

Remote Connection A network connection that uses a modem and phone lines instead of a direct cable. For a remote connection to work, both the server and the remote computer must have Domino installed. In addition, each one must have a modem and must be attached to a phone line.

When you work on a computer that's attached to the network with cables, the mail you send and the documents you create and update are immediately transferred and updated on the server. However, when you work remotely, you must first create copies (or replicas) of the databases you want to use on your remote computer and save them to your local hard disk.

When you first copy (or *replicate*) the databases, they match the databases on the server exactly. As you work on the copied databases though, they begin to differ from the databases on the server. Not only are you making changes to your copy of the database, but other users are making changes to the original database back at the office. That's why remote connections are necessary.

When you connect remotely to the server, Domino locates the changed databases and updates them with your changes (your new mail, newly created documents, and edited or deleted documents, for example). And of course, Domino also updates your databases to reflect the changes other people have made to the original databases.

CONFIGURING FOR THE MODEM

Before you can connect to the network, you must modify some settings in your computer. The changes you need to make include enabling the communications port, setting up your modem, entering the server in your address book, and setting up Domino for Remote Mail.

Disconnect Call Waiting? When working with a modem, you use a phone line that's normally used for verbal (voice) communication. Therefore, you should disconnect such phone services as call waiting so that your connection will not be interrupted and terminated.

SETTING THE PORT

You use communications ports to connect to the network. When working at the office, as you have throughout this book, you use the LAN port. When working remotely, you use a communications port such as COM1 or COM2. To set the port (let Domino know which port you're using), follow these steps:

1. Choose File, Tools, User Preferences. The User Preferences dialog box appears.
2. Choose the Ports category (bottom left of the dialog box), and the Ports options shown in Figure 26.1 appear.

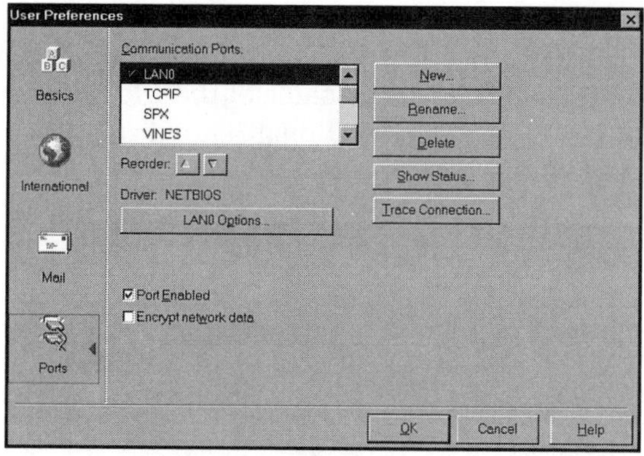

FIGURE 26.1 You must set the port before you can use a remote connection.

3. In the Communication Ports list, select the COM port to which your phone line is attached.
4. Select the Port Enabled check box.
5. Click OK to implement these settings and close the User Preferences dialog box. Alternatively, you can set additional options for your modem, as explained in the next section.

Encrypt? Click the Encrypt network data check box if you're transferring highly sensitive data and you do not want anyone to tap into it. Note, however, that using this option slows down the speed of the transmission and increases the chances of transmission errors and terminations.

You can—and should—also set your modem speed, dialing mode, and modem type, as well as a few other options from the User Preferences dialog box. To configure additional options, perform these steps:

1. In the User Preferences dialog box, click the *XXX* Options button (where *XXX* is the name of the selected port, as in COM2 Options). The Additional Setup dialog box appears (see Figure 26.2).

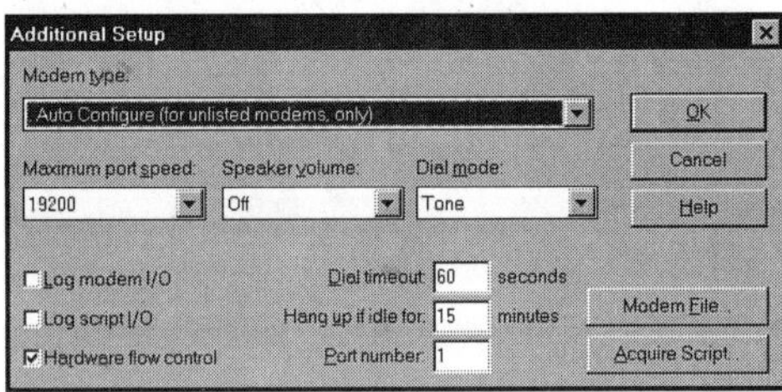

FIGURE 26.2 Configure specific settings for your modem.

2. In the Modem type list box, select the type of modem you're using.
3. Set the rest of the options. Several are explained in Table 26.1.
4. Click OK to close the Additional Setup dialog box, and then click OK again to close the User Preferences dialog box.

Table 25.1 Modem Settings

Setting	Description
Maximum port speed	Set the maximum bps (baud per second) speed your modem can use, such as 14.4, 19.2, or 38.4. (The setting 38.4 represents the port speed; use it if your modem is 28.8 bps.)
Speaker volume	Set the volume to off, low, medium, or high. The sounds you'll hear are the dial tone, the dialing, and the two modems communicating. It's a good idea to at least keep the setting on low so you can tell whether your modem is connecting and when in the sequence there's a problem (for example, if there's no dial tone or no communication between modems).
Dial mode	Indicate whether your phone uses Tone or Pulse dialing.
Dial timeout	Enter a number of seconds for Domino to continue to try dialing before hanging up.
Hang up if idle for	Enter the number of minutes of no activity that Domino should wait before hanging up.

Setting a Location

You must set up a location when using a remote connection. For example, you can use *Travel* or *Home* instead of the Office location that you've used throughout this book. The only difference between Travel and Home is in the way you set them up. You can, for example, set up the Travel location so that you can use your calling card number when you're in a hotel or remote office location. Additionally, you can set up the Home location with permanent settings for dial out numbers, area codes, and so on (but Travel location settings will change).

To set a location, click the location button in the Status bar (the second box from the right end) and choose either Home or Travel. Alternatively, you can choose File, Mobile, Choose Current Location, select the location from a list, and click OK.

Location Settings You should ask your Domino administrator for help setting up the location options if they are not already set. Creating locations is beyond the scope of this book.

Creating a Server Connection

Another setting you must complete includes the connection to the server. You'll need to know the exact name of the server, as well as the phone number you need to connect to the modem on the server. You can get both from your Domino Administrator. Follow these steps to create the server connection.

1. Choose File, Mobile, Server Phone Numbers. Your Address Book database appears in the Server/Connections view.
2. Choose Create, Server Connection. The Server Connection sheet appears (see Figure 26.3).
3. In the **Connection type** area, confirm or select Dialup Modem.
4. In the brackets next to **Server name**, enter the exact name of your server.
5. In the **Area code** brackets, enter the server's area code.
6. In the **Phone number** brackets, enter the server's phone number.
7. Choose File, Save to save the information, and then choose File, Close to close this sheet.
8. Close the Address Book database.

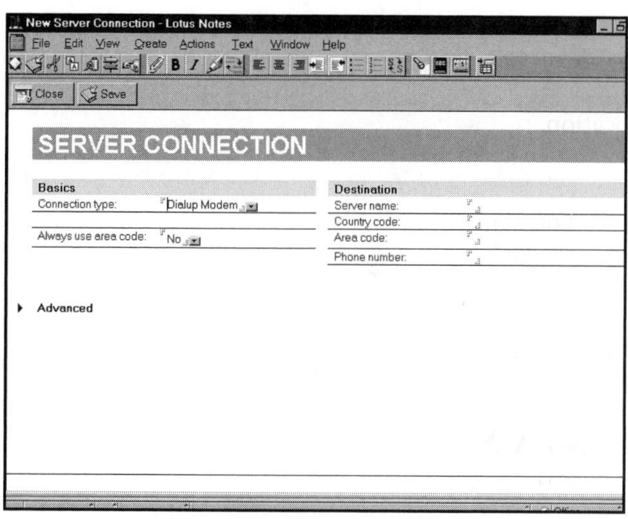

FIGURE 26.3 Set up your server connection

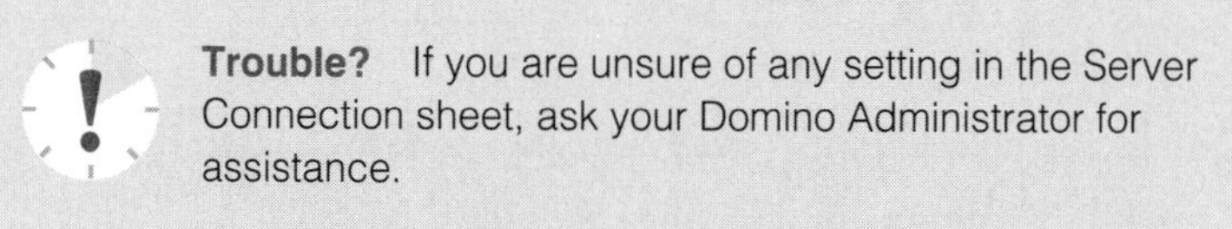

Trouble? If you are unsure of any setting in the Server Connection sheet, ask your Domino Administrator for assistance.

CONNECTING TO THE NETWORK

Connecting to the network from a remote computer is simply a matter of calling the server. Domino takes care of the connection details so you can continue with your work. Disconnecting is also easy; however, make sure you save and close all databases before you disconnect from the network.

To call the network server, follow these steps:

1. Choose File, Mobile, Call Server. The Call Server dialog box appears.

2. In the list of servers, select the server.

3. (Optional) Make any last-minute or temporary changes to the port, timeout, or call setup settings described in Table 26.1.
4. Click Auto Dial. Domino dials the server and connects your remote computer to the network, from which you can replicate mail and databases.

To disconnect from the server, choose File, Mobile, Hang Up.

REPLICATING DATABASES

You can *replicate*, or copy, your databases to and from the server for use when you're working remotely. Doing so ensures that you'll always have up-to-date material with which to work and that your coworkers will have access to changes you make to the databases as well.

Follow the steps below to replicate a Domino database:

1. After connecting to the server, select the database on your workspace by clicking it.
2. Choose File, Replication, Replicate, and the Replicate database dialog box appears (see Figure 26.4).

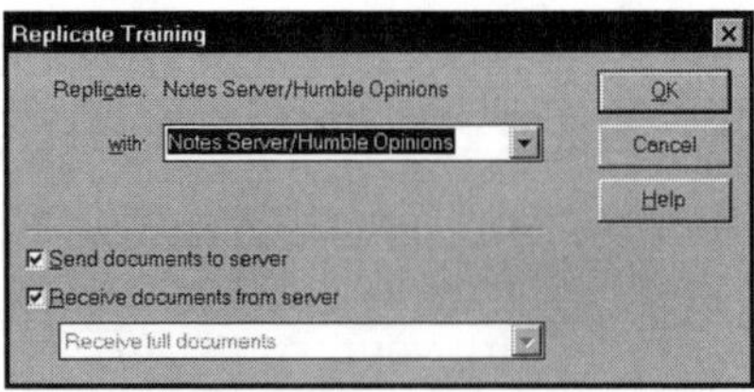

FIGURE 26.4 The Replicate database dialog box.

3. In the with text box, select a different server from the list if you don't want to replicate to the currently selected server.

4. Select the Send documents to server check box if you want to replicate to the server; select Receive documents from server if you want to replicate to your workstation. If you choose to receive documents, use the drop-down list to indicate whether you want to receive full documents or document summaries (document summaries contain only basic document information such as the title and author).
5. Click **OK**.

SENDING AND RECEIVING MAIL

Domino's replicate feature also works in the mailbox. When you replicate mail, you send mail to and receive mail from the network using a remote connection, and Domino updates your mailbox accordingly.

To replicate mail, follow these steps:

1. After connecting to the network, choose the Replicator tab.
2. Choose the Send & Receive Mail tool button. Domino sends your mail to the server and receives any new mail.

Send Only If you want to send outgoing mail without receiving incoming mail, select the check box to the left of the Send outgoing mail icon and click the Start tool button. Domino sends your mail to the network.

Installation

This appendix walks you through installing Lotus Notes to a local area network (LAN) workstation running Windows 95 or NT 4.

Before you attempt to install Lotus Notes, make sure these three things are true:

- The workstation is connected to a server with cables or by phone lines.
- The network server is up and running, and the Domino server is up and running.
- The Domino server contains an active account for you, which was set up by your System Administrator.

Once you have verified those things, you need to temporarily disable any screen savers and virus-detection software, and make sure no programs are running on the workstation. Any time you need additional information during the software installation, ask your system administrator.

Installing Notes Client on a Windows 95 Workstation

If the operating system you use with your workstation is Windows 95, you can install Notes to that workstation and use Notes in conjunction with the many benefits and features of Windows 95. To install Notes on a Windows 95 workstation, follow these steps:

1. From the Windows 95 desktop, click the Start button and choose Run.

2. Insert the Lotus CD or insert the floppy disk labelled Disk 1 in the drive. Then enter the command **drive:\directory\install**. For example, type **d:\win32\install\install** and press Enter. Insert new disks in the floppy drive as prompted. Lotus copies files to your hard disk and then displays the Welcome to Lotus Notes Install Program dialog box.

3. Enter your name and company name and choose Next. The Confirm Names dialog box appears.

4. Click Yes to confirm the names, or click No and re-enter them. The Install Options dialog box appears.

It Already Exists If a copy of Notes already exists on your hard drive, Lotus displays the Multiple Copies of Notes for Windows dialog box, in which you can choose to overwrite that copy. Choose Next to overwrite the original copy. If, on the other hand, you don't want to overwrite the original, you can exit the installation, go to the previous dialog box, or get help.

5. Choose the Standard Install option and click Next. The Select Program Folder dialog box appears.

6. Click Next to install Notes to the default folder (Lotus Applications), or select another folder in the folder list. The Begin Copying Files dialog box appears.

7. Click Yes, and Notes begins copying files to your hard disk. The Lotus Install-Transferring Files dialog box tracks the progress of the installation. You can choose Cancel at any time to stop the installation.

8. When the installation is complete, Lotus displays the Install Complete dialog box. Click Done to return to the Windows 95 desktop.

What Do I Do Now? If you receive an error message at any time during installation, contact your Domino administrator for help.

To start Notes, click the Start button on the taskbar and choose Programs. In the Lotus Applications folder (or the folder you installed to if you chose something other than the default), choose Lotus Notes.

The first time you start Notes after installation, the program connects to the server to access settings and options. When setup is complete, Notes displays a message telling you that setup was successful.

Installing Notes on an NT 4 Workstation

Installing the Notes Client to an NT 4 Workstation should be exactly like installing to a Windows 95 machine. Make sure your system adminstrator has granted you permission to access the network and the Domino server. Then proceed as previously described for Windows 95.

INDEX

SYMBOLS

A

B

C

D

E

G-H

I

J-L

M

N

O

P

Q-R

S

T

U

V

W